# PROCEEDINGS OF THE MODERN LANGUAGE ASSOCIATION NEOCLASSICISM CONFERENCES, 1967-1968

EDITED BY
PAUL J. KORSHIN
UNIVERSITY OF PENNSYLVANIA

AMS PRESS
NEW YORK

Copyright © 1970 AMS Press, Inc.

International Standard Book Number: 0-404-04348-8

Library of Congress Catalog Card Number: 76-124161

Manufactured in the United States of America

AMS PRESS, INC.
NEW YORK, N.Y. 10003

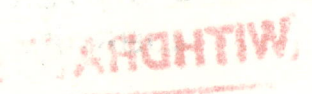

INTRODUCTION

The Proceedings and Bibliography published in this volume had very modest origins. The first Neoclassicism Conference had its conception in late spring 1967 when the editor and several friends, feeling that the larger groups and sections at the Modern Language Association Annual Meeting provided very little opportunity for interchange of ideas and open discussion, decided to organize a conference for one year to see if such a small meeting might provoke the interest of people in our field. Though the organizers were, at that time, all located in the northeast, there was immediate favorable response from scholars in different regions of the country and, when Conference 28 ultimately had its brief lifespan at a meeting room in the Palmer House, some sixty people crowded a small, uncomfortable room to hear Professors Dussinger, Jackson, McIntosh, and Weinbrot debate recent interpretations of the term "Augustan" and the implications of literary terminology for eighteenth-century studies. There were interesting, challenging contributions from certain members of the audience, more than enough to persuade the panelists at the Conference that they had enjoyed a modest success and to encourage them to try again the following year.

Thus the Conference, converted into a Seminar by one of the MLA's puzzling changes in nomenclature, was rechartered for the 1968 Annual Meeting. The organizers agreed to adopt a more recognizable title which might, if necessary, be used again in future years, so "Problems of Neoclassicism" was chosen. The shift from "Augustan" to "neoclassic," while it represented a departure from the aura of elegance which is thought by some to surround the Augustan Age, seemed advisable at the time because the term "Neoclassicism" has traditionally been associated with literary theory and history in this period of English literature. And so the Seminar continued to be described, in its third year of existence, by this title (with a different subtitle). It is difficult accurately to describe the purpose of a shifting group like this one, whose existence from year to year depends upon the interest of several dozen scholars and the willingness of one of them to assemble a panel and to chair the meeting. But it has always been evident to the panel members at these meetings that the scholarly journals and the large paper-oriented meetings dealing with the eighteenth century do not provide adequate facilities for the informal presentation of new theories currently being explored or developed by scholars in the field. The journal provides an outlet for published research; the large meeting an opportunity to present sophisticated studies to a large audience.

But the small conference or Seminar may, under the proper circumstances, allow scholars to discuss work in progress, often nearly completed, with a knowledgeable, critical audience. But I doubt that any participants have seriously considered the Neoclassicism Conferences as "work-in-progress" sessions, in the sense of being meetings for the discussion of research opportunities in the field. For three-fourths of the panelists in the first two years have chosen to have their papers, in every case considerably enlarged from their informal oral presentation, printed in these Proceedings. This is a high proportion, probably above that of most meetings, to appear in print at all. It is a sign that such conferences as these, particularly if they can find a willing publisher, can fulfill a significant role in literary studies.

Eighteenth-century studies have not been colonized with the kind of zeal familiar to other branches of literary scholarship, both as regards the number of specialized journals and so far as periodic meetings and associations are concerned. There are the quadrennial International Conferences on the Enlightenment and, in the United States, a nascent association for eighteenth-century studies, but the kind of meetings which are frequent in other fields are incidental in this one. Perhaps this may not always be so. Perhaps, on the other hand, it should remain so. Nevertheless, as many regular participants in MLA Annual Meetings will doubtless agree, the large association meeting has become increasingly less desirable for the discussion of ideas. Hence it is tempting to think that something like these conferences, whether less informal or larger, may in the next decade supersede the impersonality of crowded corridors and the discomfort of hotel meeting rooms. The two-day conference sponsored last fall by _Eighteenth-Century Studies_ for the University of California may be a prototype of what we may hope for in the future. Within this context, I think, the Neoclassicism Conference (or Seminar) can continue to furnish a forum for discussion of important or controversial problems within the field of eighteenth-century studies.

The contents of this volume, then, which vary from the informality of Professor Hart and the precise brevity of Professor McIntosh to the scholarly thoroughness of Professor Weinbrot and Professor Guilhamet, represent some work which is still in progress, and some which has been completed. The idea of each meeting was to encourage individual scholars to comment upon different aspects of the same topic, which the contributors have accomplished with considerable success. The Bibliography, though it is far from complete, is sufficiently large itself to indicate the scholarly vitality of the subject at hand.

Paul J. Korshin

Villanova, Pa.
15 October 1969

## TABLE OF CONTENTS

| | |
|---|---:|
| Introduction, by Paul J. Korshin, University of Pennsylvania | iii |
| Program, Conference 28, "Recent Definitions of 'Augustan'" | 2 |
| On the Discrimination of Augustan Satires, by Howard D. Weinbrot, University of Wisconsin | 4 |
| Satire: An Augustan Idea of Disorder, by Wallace Jackson, Duke University | 12 |
| The Scheduled Quest, by Carey McIntosh, University of Rochester | 26 |
| Program, Seminar 64, "Problems of Neoclassicism: Theories of Imitation" | 31 |
| Imitation and Originality in the Poems of Thomas Gray, by Leon M. Guilhamet, Yale University | 33 |
| Augustan Imitation: The Role of the Original, by Howard D. Weinbrot, University of Wisconsin | 53 |
| Particular and General Truth: Some Speculative Footnotes to Scott Elledge, by Jeffrey Hart, Dartmouth College | 71 |
| The Literature of Neoclassicism, 1920-1968: A Bibliography, compiled by Paul J. Korshin, University of Pennsylvania | 85 |

1967 NEOCLASSICISM CONFERENCE

CONFERENCE 28: RECENT DEFINITIONS OF "AUGUSTAN"

Discussion leader, PAUL J. KORSHIN, Univ. of Pennsylvania

Thursday, 28 December 1967, 10:30-11:45 A.M.

I. Opening Remarks

II. Introductory Statements

1. Howard D. Weinbrot, Univ. of Wisconsin, "The Discrimination of Augustan Satires." (5 min.)
   Summary. Any synoptic definition of Augustan satire is likely to raise more problems than it pretends to solve. The discrimination of Augustan satires is a more fruitful approach and, because of its variety and flexibility, more properly "Augustan." Some of these modes include the largely punitive and comic, harsh satiric and more moderate epistolary formal verse satire, both of which include varying degrees of affirmation, and the still harsher revelatory or apocalyptic satires, in which the satirist aims primarily at exposing rather than correcting vice.

2. Wallace Jackson, Duke Univ., "Augustan Satire: An Idea of Disorder." (5 min.)
   Summary. Augustan poetic satire locates as the object of attack an idea of disorder consistent with Locke's definition of judgment, Addison's of mixed wit, and Dr. Johnson's of the discordia concors. Such terms define the Augustan satirist's exploitation of the comedy of false relations and are relevant to imagery, to rhetorical and episodic patterns, and to the typology of the satiric victim.

3. R. Carey McIntosh, Univ. of Rochester, "The Scheduled Quest: An Augustan Genre." (5 min.)
   Summary. The Augustans did their best work in didactic genres, and characteristic petit-genres of the eighteenth century are sustained by the delight of instruction, by passionate moral concern. For example, the impulse to survey mankind, tendentiously, works as a structural principle in many of the finest Augustan writings, and crops up unexpectedly throughout our period.

4. John A. Dussinger, Univ. of Illinois, "The Relevance of 'Augustan' to Eighteenth-Century Prose Fiction." (5 min.)
   Summary. The term "Augustan" or "neoclassical" is not very suitable to describe the dominant prose fiction of the eighteenth century. A new phenomenology is implicit in the

writings of Defoe, Richardson, Fielding, and Sterne, which outstrips any principle of mimetic order from the ancients, and the representational techniques developed bear little relationship to classical models, despite Fielding's professed intentions.

III. Discussion (55 min.)

## ON THE DISCRIMINATION OF AUGUSTAN SATIRES

By Howard D. Weinbrot

Many recent discussions of satire imply that satire is a monolithic genre, one that can be characterized by means of a capsule-description or mini-definition. These generally tell us that there are "standard procedures of satire"; or that "satire consists of" certain traits; or "satire is a work so organized that" specified things happen; or "satire is the genre most preoccupied with" a few selected themes; or, "the satiric form is anything that" includes what the critic observes that it should include.[1] Such comments, however, are unfaithful to the complexity of satiric forms from, say, 1660 to 1750. It would be more "Augustan" to abandon a synoptic view of satire in favor of the discrimination of Augustan satires.

For example, Mac Flecknoe (1682) is essentially comic towards its audience and punitive towards its victim. Shadwell is easily defeated and is never a threat to the organizing threads of the universe. Hence it is a "harmless War with words" that Panton wages (1.84), and Shadwell learns "Pangs without birth, and fruitless Industry" (1. 148).[2] Though one assumes that good writers are preferable to bad, Dryden focuses on abuse not instruction.

The Dunciad (1743), in contrast, is apocalyptic or revelatory -- I borrow the terms from Section I of A Tale of a Tub (1704)[3] -- and aims not so much at punishment or correction of vice, but at portrayal of the death of Western culture. If the norms in Mac Flecknoe were submerged, those in the Dunciad are overt but extremely tenuous, as even the light of wit, a projection from God, is put out. The poet must resort to mention of a few noble figures like Handel or Swift, whereas in his formal verse satire we see comparable figures either living and acting in Pope's home, or having some demonstrable, if limited, influence upon life. He also implicitly invokes the distant Greek, Roman, or Miltonic literary traditions through his own style and allusions and, ultimately, invokes the dying voice of the poet himself, whose final plea for light is denied in the poem and, paradoxically, granted by posterity. Nevertheless, the dunces break Pegasus' neck, and torture, kill, and mince the Muses, as "Universal Darkness buries All." Mac Flecknoe shows us a triumphant satirist and a "harmless war with words"; the Dunciad reveals a defeated satirist and a cataclysmic war.

Though different in many ways, A Tale of a Tub and Gulliver's Travels (1726) are also revelatory, and depict the terrible world both around and within us. The chief target of Gulliver's Travels, for instance, is the depravity of human nature. Gulliver's allusion to Sinon, in Book IV,[4] illustrates this: Sinon is the Greek bearing the gift of the Trojan horse; he insists that though Fortune has made him miserable, she has not made him false and a liar. Gulliver is not only associated with a liar[5] but, of greater importance, with a horse and a long, and unsuccessful attempt to destroy the walls of a great city. Subterfuge is necessary. Thus, to apply the allusion to the reader, it will be the apparently innocent travel-book that we will invite into our "city" and that will (Swift hopes) break down the walls of our pride; otherwise the normative -- or rather the ideal -- purity of the Houyhnhnms "love thy neighbor as thyself" is impossible. Troy must be ruined before Rome can be built.

Revelatory satire, then, is primarily concerned with depicting a grim situation rather than both attacking vice and presenting a clearly workable norm. Augustan formal verse satire, however, adopts the latter method. This mode is generally in heroic couplets, is based in part upon the varied examples of Horace, Persius, and Juvenal and -- as enunciated in Dryden's well known "Discourse concerning the Original and Progress of Satyr" (1693) -- includes attacks upon a specific vice and praise of its opposite virtue.[6] This scheme offers tremendous variety for the use of norms. The praise might be implicit in the vice attacked, as in Juvenal's Sixth Satire, on women; or it might emerge as one major and one or more minor statements, as in Johnson's London (1738); perhaps, as in several of Pope's satires, the speaker and a small group of friends embody the good life; there might also be a long series of attacks followed by a shorter section recommending the opposite virtue, as in the Vanity of Human Wishes (1749); or, as in Edward Young's first six satires in the Love of Fame (1725-28), the poet might use interlocking sections of praise and blame, whereas in the seventh he turns to overt panegyric of Walpole and George I.

Indeed, Young's Love of Fame, Pope's Imitations of Horace (1733-1739) and his Ethic Epistles (1731-1735), and Johnson's London all offer norms whose presence and varying degrees of hope and efficacy are demanded by the form itself. These poems attack abuses in the national or human situation and insist that, in some way, one may either correct, punish, or escape from them. Of course here too they work in different ways. The Love of Fame offers so many facile norms that its credibility as a satire is threatened, and Pope's Epilogue to the Satires (1738) offers so little hope for the practicability of its norms that it exists at the furthest end of the spectrum of formal verse satire. But it is one nevertheless: Pope balances the portrait of the perverted court heaven (<u>Dialogue</u> I, ll. 90-104) with a vision of the true Heaven (<u>Dialogue</u> II, ll. 232-247). One sees protest plus achievable (if neglected) norms in the <u>Epilogue</u>, but protest plus darkness in the <u>Dunciad</u>. The poet is still alive, if ultimately silent, in the former; but asleep and a victim of Dulness in the latter. One poem ends in Britain's spiritual defeat, the other in universal darkness; one shows the inability of the good man to affect the vicious about him and, consequently, falling back on a protective Heaven; the other shows all communication cut off as God's creating word is nullified. Even <u>London</u> which (heretically) portrays an ineffectual God in that city (ll. 194-209), also portrays a viable norm for man in this world (ll. 210-223), and shows his refusal to be defeated, since the poem ends with the vigorous propagation of satire. In formal verse satire achievement of the norm is difficult -- sometimes incredibly so -- but possible; there is generally a living example and often a benevolent, actively engaged God. He may reject the depraved world but, like God in the Biblical tale, He preserves order as long as there is one good man. In the revelatory <u>Dunciad</u> the last good man dies with the final word of the poem; and in comic satire like <u>Mac Flecknoe</u> normative benevolence is submerged under comic hostility.

An important difference between revelatory and formal verse satire may be seen by contrasting <u>Gulliver's Travels</u> and the <u>Vanity of Human Wishes</u>. In both the Christian must recognize and accept his original sin before he can hope to ameliorate it. But the methods of the satirists are different. Johnson overtly raises these questions: "Where then shall Hope and Fear their objects find? / Must dull Suspence corrupt the stagnant mind?" (ll. 343-344). And he just as overtly answers them: "Enquirer, cease, petitions yet remain, / Which heav'n may hear, nor deem religion vain" (ll. 349-350). The norm is clear; so is the result of adherence to it: "celestial wisdom calms the mind, / And makes the happiness she does not find" (ll. 367-368).[7] But this wisdom evokes unhappiness in Gulliver; he does not know that he cannot live up to it; it separates him from the communion of man[8] and, for too many modern readers, even makes that wisdom suspect. In his letter to Cousin Sympson Gulliver argues that the numerous reformations he hopes to effect "were plainly deducible from the Precepts delivered in my Book."[9] The formal verse satirist would probably not have left these for an uncertain deduction.

Formal verse satire itself falls into several categories, among them the harsher "satire" which emphasizes blame, and the more moderate "epistle" which emphasizes praise. Numerous major scholars and editors of Horace made this distinction and helped pass it on to Pope and his contemporaries. Julius Caesar Scaliger, for instance, observes of Horace's epistles: "just as medicine either preserves from illness or carries illness off, these epistles propose those things with which we may abstain from vice, satire fights with those by which vices are driven out."[10] Daniel Heinsius also distinguishes between satires and epistles, and believes that the plan of Horace was to join "truth which is the soul of philosophy, and freedom which is the chief virtue of satire." Hence he teaches virtue with different approaches; in the satires "by criticizing, in the later books which we now call epistles" by hortatory or doctrinal means, by "precept and teaching."[11] In order to illustrate this distinction in practice, I would like to posit a spectrum for four of Pope's formal verse satires: the Epistle to Bathurst (1733) is near the mild epistolary end; the Epistle to Dr. Arbuthnot (1735) closer to the center of the epistolary side, the First Satire of the Second Book of Horace (to Fortescue) (1733) on the "satiric" side, and the two Dialogues (1738) near the extremely harsh end. A brief examination of each adversary's concluding remarks should explain the poem's approximate position.

In Bathurst Pope persuades a rational man to return to an orthodox Christian viewpoint; Bathurst's final word is "Agreed" (l. 338). In Arbuthnot a distinguished Doctor learns that Pope's medicinal satire is necessary; he helps to destroy the chief enemy and, in so doing, becomes a satirist himself. Though this poem is harsher than Bathurst, we again see the rational man convinced by the satirist: "Thus far was right, the rest belongs to Heaven" (l. 419).[12]

In Fortescue we have moved firmly onto the satiric side; here the adversary can only give conditional acceptance to Pope's moral pleas, and agrees that "the case is altered" (l. 154) only when it seems that Pope has won the approval of established power. Then "My Lords the Judges [will] laugh, and you're dismissed" (l. 156). With the two Dialogues, this dubious alliance -- or fantasy regarding one -- has collapsed. In the epistles and the more moderate satire the adversary represents an audience of reasonable men; when he is convinced we are as well. But no such rational man exists in the Dialogues. In the first the Impertinent Censurer concludes with a corrupt vision of a heaven in which court sycophants thrive, while Pope is forced to speak grotesque lines which, properly, belong to his enemy, and to offer a feeble one-couplet disclaimer in rebuttal. In the second all common ground is gone; Pope must find solace in Heaven not Britain, as the adversary closes his mind to Pope's arguments and urges him to write more generalizing poems like the Essay on Man (1733-1734). The dialogue, a metaphor for human communication, breaks down, as rational man and rational audience disappear. Pope is the "Last of Britons" and refuses to write any more satire. The poems, then, get progressively grimmer as we move along this satiric spectrum of formal verse satires, and the relationship between satirist and adversary, and the degree of praise found in each poem, signals that change.

These rough discriminations between comic and punitive, apocalyptic or revelatory, and satiric and epistolary formal verse satires can only be a beginning for more intense inquiry into the varied Augustan modes of satire. I hope that it will also contribute to the decline of the largely unhistorical synoptic definition.

University of Wisconsin

NOTES

1. For the full context of these remarks, see Bernard N. Schilling, Dryden and the Conservative Myth (New Haven, 1961), p. 11; Edward W. Rosenheim, Jr., Swift and the Satirist's Art (Chicago, 1963), p. 31; Paul Fussell, The Rhetorical World of Augustan Humanism (New York, 1965), p. 112; Sheldon Sacks, Fiction and the Shape of Belief (Berkeley and Los Angeles, 1964), p. 26; Ronald Paulson, Satire and the Novel in Eighteenth-Century England (New Haven, 1967), p. 4; Paulson, The Fictions of Satire (Baltimore, 1967), pp. 6-7. Leonard Feinberg notes that, however brilliant a critic might be, his attempt to define "satire" is likely to fail, since satire "offers so many varieties of structure that by careful selection one can prove almost anything he sets out to prove": "Satire: The Inadequacy of Recent Definitions," in Genre, I (1968), 32. See also Patricia Meyer Spacks, "Some Reflections on Satire," ibid., 13-30.

2. The Poems of John Dryden, ed. James Kinsley (Oxford, 1958), I, 267, 269. For a study of Mac Flecknoe as punitive and comic, see Ian Jack, Augustan Satire (Oxford, 1952), pp. 43-52. Rosenheim makes similar remarks: Swift and the Satirist's Art, pp. 13, 24, 25.

3. See Swift's A Tale of a Tub, To which is added The Battle of the Books and the Mechanical Operation of the Spirit, ed., A.C. Guthkelch and D. Nichol Smith, 2nd ed. (Oxford, 1958), p. 68.

4. Gulliver's Travels, The Prose Works of Jonathan Swift, ed. Herbert J. Davis, (Oxford, 1959), XI, 292. The lines are from the Aeneid, II, 79-80:

>       ----- Nec si miserum Fortuna Sinonem
> Finxit, vanum etiam medacemque improba finget.

5. Earl R. Wasserman has recently mentioned this passage: "Surely the reader is expected to recall that Sinon was, in fact, the most heroic of liars and that through his deceitful protestation of truthfulness he persuaded the Trojans to admit another kind of fictitious horse -- to the destruction of their city": "The Limits of Allusion in The Rape of the Lock," JEGP, LXV (1966), 444. There are far too many articles on Gulliver in general and Book IV in particular to be listed here. For a

useful sample, see two anthologies: *Gulliver's Travels: An Annotated Text with Critical Essays*, ed. Robert A. Greenberg (New York, 1961); *A Case Book on Gulliver Among the Houyhnms*, ed. Milton P. Foster (New York, 1961). To these should be added R.S. Crane's important essay, "The Houyhnhnms, the Yahoos, and the History of Ideas," in *Reason and the Imagination*, ed. Joseph Mazzeo (New York, 1965), pp. 231-253 (reprinted in Ronald S. Crane, *The Idea of the Humanities* [Chicago, 1967], II, 261-282). Crane lists several of the "soft-line" essays on pp. 231-232, n. 2. For other relevant remarks, see Edward W. Rosenheim, Jr., "The Fifth Voyage of Lemuel Gulliver: A Footnote," *MP*, LX (1962), 103-119; Paulson, *The Fictions of Satire*, pp. 162-185; Donald J. Greene, "On Swift's 'Scatological' Poems," *Sewanee Review*, LXXV (1967), 688-689.

6. See *The Essays of John Dryden*, ed. W.P. Ker (Oxford, 1926), II, 102-105. For further discussion of the popularity of Dryden's concept, see Howard D. Weinbrot, "The Pattern of Formal Verse Satire in the Restoration and the Eighteenth Century," *PMLA*, LXXX (1965), 394-401. This article, together with much of the information and analysis presented above, may also be found in Weinbrot, *The Formal Strain: Studies in Augustan Imitation and Satire* (Chicago, 1969).

7. *Samuel Johnson: Poems*, The Yale Edition of the Works of Samuel Johnson, vol. VI, ed. E.L. McAdam and George Milne (New Haven, 1964), pp. 107-109.

8. "To this Hour," Gulliver says of his wife and children, "they dare not presume to touch my Bread, or drink out of the same Cup" (pp. 289-290). Herbert Davis observes that an Anglican priest could not "use such words unconsciously, and such a one as Swift must have been willing to allow these overtones to remain -- the bread and the cup; and even the word *presume*, from the opening of the prayer before the act of communion; even the phrase *suffer them*, of the children's eating in the same room; even the tone ringing so clearly in the phrase *to this hour*. There is here . . . evidence enough of Swift's intention to emphasize Gulliver's complete estrangement from the human race, his inability to live any longer in communion with his own kind": "Swift's Use of Irony," in Maximillian E. Novak and Herbert J. Davis, *The Uses of Irony: Papers on Defoe and Swift Read at a Clark Library Seminar*, April 2, 1966 (Los Angeles, William Andrews Clark Memorial Library, 1966), pp. 55-56.

9. *Gulliver's Travels*, op. cit., 7.

10. *Poetices libri septem*, 5th ed. (Heidelberg, 1617), p. 808. "Nam quemadmodum medecina aut preseruat a morbis, aut eos tollit: ita Epistolae proponunt ea, quib a vitio abstineamus, Satyra illus pugnat, quibus vitia extirpentur." Pope told Spence that Scaliger's "*Poetics* is an exceeding useful book in its kind, and extremely well collected": *Anecdotes . . . of Books and Men. By Joseph Spence*, ed. James M. Osborn (Oxford, 1966), I, 20. Osborn notes that "Pope refers to [Scaliger's *Poetics*] in the *Narrative of Dr. Norris* (1713) and in the Preface to the *Iliad* (1715)" (*ibid.*).

11. *Quintus Horatius Flaccus. Accedunt nunc Danielis Heinsii de satyra Horatiana libri duo . . .* (Leiden 1629), p. 226. The full context is as follows: "Simul enim veritatem, quae est anima philosophiae; & libertatem, quae praecipua Satyrici est virtus, conjunxit. Quare cum diuersa ratione doceat virtutem; in prioribus, ipsis nimirum Satyrarum libris, [critically], sive reprehendendo; in posterioribus, quas Epistolas nunc dicimus, quod magis erat usitatum, [hortatory] nonnunquam, nec non alibi [doctrinally], seu praecipiendo ac docendo; in prioribus fidenter, non in mores tantum hominum, sed philosophorum quoque opiniones, plurima urbanitate, sale, lepore, dicacitate & risu incurrit; sicut in Posterioribus, nudam sine auctoritate veritatem sequitur, quam docet; quod & in principio no sine causa prositetur. Utramque autem rationem in Platone habes, ut & ordinem. Ita Socrates perpetuo fere arguit, priusquam docet. Ut in magno Alcibiade, & alibi." Pope owned a copy of Heinsius. For discussion of Pope's texts in his *Imitations of Horace*, see Bonamy Dobrée, "Pope's Horace," *Times Literary Supplement* (August 12, 1939), p. 479; Lillian D. Bloom, "Pope as Textual Critic: A Bibliographical Study of his Horatian Text," *JEGP*, XLVII (1948), 150-155; Robert W. Rogers' corrective review of Mrs. Bloom, above, *PQ*, XXVIII (1949), 397-398; *Alexander Pope: Imitations of Horace*, The Twickenham Edition of the Poems of Alexander Pope, vol. IV, ed. John Butt, 2nd ed. (London, 1953), p. xliii.

12. For the texts of these poems see *Alexander Pope: Epistles to Several Persons*, The Twickenham Edition of the Poems of Alexander Pope, Vol. III, part ii, ed. F.W. Bateson, 2nd ed. (London, 1961), p. 120; and *Imitations of Horace*, op. cit. Thomas A. Maresca has made a convincing case for attributing these lines to Arbuthnot: *Pope's Horatian Poems* (Columbus, Ohio, 1966), pp. 108-110, and p. 116, n. 36.

## SATIRE: AN AUGUSTAN IDEA OF DISORDER

### By Wallace Jackson

What I should like to do in these pages is to suggest a set of related terms expressive of an idea of disorder in the later seventeenth and early eighteenth centuries and to put this idea in relation to English satire of the period. I hope thereby to provide a dependable overview by relying upon what is extremely familiar in the literature. But before developing the function of these related terms in Augustan satire, I wish to introduce two concepts that may be known as the concordia discors and the discordia concors; the former depends upon the making of order out of the clash of contrarieties, and as such is an old and pervasive idea in the history of Western thought. The latter, however, in which I shall be especially interested, is the making of discord by putting into relation things falsely conceived as harmonious. Following Dr. Johnson, I should like to employ his definition of the discordia concors as "a combination of dissimilar images, or discovery of occult resemblances in things apparently unlike."[1] Dr. Johnson, as we know, used the term discordia concors as one of condemnation and had particularly in mind the poetry of Abraham Cowley and the metaphysical school. My purpose, however, will be to advance the proposition that the discordia concors served the ends of satire in the later seventeenth and early eighteenth centuries, and was therefore a means of manifesting a fairly consistent idea of disorder. In short, I hope to show that the discordia concors and some related terms offered by both Locke and Addison define the very nature and character of that disorder which is the object of satiric rebuke within the period. Thus let me make my intentions clear: the concordia discors, as it invokes the principle that contrarieties make harmony, offered to the early eighteenth century a system or pattern of order that could apparently be applied to a very large area of human experience. The discordia concors, on the other hand, offered the very terms in which disorder was most clearly, most extensively apprehended. The former served as a basis for an idea of order stated in some, at least, of the major works of the time; the latter, on the contrary, provided a basis for the concept of disorder characterized in some, at least, of the major works of satire produced at the same time. Together both terms offer a curiously paradoxical perspective on the human condition and suggest the necessity for an historical awareness that must ultimately reckon with the relation of the one to the other.

With the first concept, the concordia discors, I shall be only briefly concerned; my purpose is to glance merely at the concept in some of the non-satiric literature of the period. The discordia concors, however, implies the obverse or darker side of the idea of order; it suggests an extensive distrust of the union of those characteristics or qualities that are radically dissimilar, and the implications of this Augustan idea of disorder have considerable bearing on the literature of the entire century. I am, however, promising somewhat more than I shall perform, but I believe I can indicate the relevance of the discordia concors to other values within the eighteenth century, values that had the effect of somewhat delimiting and restricting the range of inquiry carried on especially by English critics and literary theorists later in the century.

In the first epistle of An Essay on Man, Pope remarks as he brings the epistle to a close, "All Discord, Harmony, not Understood." The line expresses a major theme within the poem, the pervasive believe that it is the tension of opposing forces that makes unity, and as Maynard Mack remarks, all the "abstract pieces of his argument Pope catches up like his predecessors in the metaphor of harmony-from-discord that has influenced Western thinking for more than twenty centuries."[2] Such is the triumph of cosmos over chaos, a triumph that Pope's last work, the new Dunciad of 1743 would reverse. But, in 1733, it was this metaphor that enabled Pope to take account of the observable heterogeneity and conflict of things and to reconcile them. So, too, did Shaftesbury in "The Moralists, A Philosophical Rhapsody," argue that the world's beauty is "founded thus on contrarieties, whilst from such various and disagreeing principles a universal concord is established."[3] The concept of concordia discors is also given important place in William King's Essay on the Origin of Evil in which he proposes the necessity for God's creation of a "contrariety of motions" to secure "the greatest good and the least possible evil in the material world."[4] Professor Wasserman has found evidence also that the subtler language of Denham's Cooper's Hill and Pope's Windsor Forest depends, in his words, "upon the complex syntax of concordia discors," and that, finally, "the system of contrariety provided a viable pattern of thought that could be applied to the entire range of human experience."[5] Professor Mack has confirmed this view in his remark that the fellowship and the hierarchy implicit in the concept of the great chain of being, so important to Pope's conception of universal order in the Essay,"are but other ways of visualizing the Heraclitean concors discordia, where every member of the universal orchestra contributes something and all are reconciled by a Providence that both composes and conducts."[6] Moreover, "the equilibrium of opposites by which God established a cosmos out of the chaos of the elements must be matched in the individual's life by an equilibrium of passions," and this "same kind of creative equilibrium must be realized in the societies of the civil state and ultimately in the imaginative act whereby 'the whole worlds of Reason, life, and sense' are grasped and held 'in one close system of benevolence.'"[7] The concept of an equilibrium achieved through the clash of opposites, and the harmonizing of them, dates back at least to the third of Plotinus' _Enneads_. Professor Lovejoy cites Plotinus to the effect that "'difference carried to its maximum _is_ opposition.' And since to contain and to engender difference, 'to produce otherness,' is the very essence of the creative World-soul, 'it will necessarily do this in the maximal degree, and therefore produce things opposed to one another . . . . Only so will its perfection be realized.'"[8]

Yet despite the importance attributed by Shaftesbury, by Pope, and by King to the concept of concordia discors, despite the occasional reiteration of the theme in such minor figures as Henry Brooke, and William Mason, and Richard Graves later in the century, it was apparent by mid-century, or even earlier, that the concordia discors was disintegrating "from a vital harmony dependent upon contrariety into a standard of some difference plus some uniformity."[9] My brief recapitulation of it here is intended only to rehearse its currency in the early years of the eighteenth century, and to suggest that it provided a basis for an idea of order to which some extensive credence was given. But it is not, as I have indicated, a theory of order with which I shall be principally concerned. On the contrary, it is of what might be called the obverse of this idea, the discordia concors, that I shall speak.

The argument I should like to make is that the discordia concors provided a basis for satire in the later seventeenth and early eighteenth centuries, and that it did so by exploiting the comedy implicit in the false unification of contrarieties or incongruities, of antitheses related, of discord perceived as accord. My argument, therefore, to some extend depends upon the notion that the concordia discors could be, if so I may put it, subverted to the purposes of satire. The discordia concors defines an idea of disorder by turning the concordia discors topsy-turvy. But I should like here to put the principle of discordia concors into relation with two other terms that will be of especial use in defining the idea of disorder. The first is that of the failed judgment, and I take my definition inferentially from Locke's definition of judgment in An Essay Concerning Human Understanding. Judgment, he says, lies "in separating carefully, one from another, ideas wherein can be found the least difference, thereby to avoid being misled by similitude, and by affinity to take one thing for another."[10] In other words, although Locke is quite clear, judgment lies in keeping disparate things apart, and to fail in judgment is to put things that are different together. When in 1711, in Spectator 62, Addison comes to consider Locke's definition, he develops the term mixed wit, in which, as he explains, the "foundations are laid partly in falsehood and partly in truth. Reason puts in her claim for one half of it, and extravagance for the other."[11] And in this regard Addison cites Cowley as an example of a poet who used mixed wit, just indeed as Dr. Johnson was to cite Cowley considerably later as an example of the poet who employs the discordia concors. Now it seems to me that these three terms have a common basis, for the failed judgment, the mixed wit, and the discordia concors all define the making of harmony from the union of things that are disharmonious. Each condemns muddled or inappropriate relations, the union of the incongruous or the outré. Addison and Johnson do so directly, Locke does so by implication. Thus from 1690 to 1778 there is a certain common agreement in the censure of false relationships, and there is more than a fair consistency in the terms that are so employed. To this argument I might add the authority of each of these men during the period, an authority presumably substantiating the best thought of the time in such matters as these.

I should like further to suggest that the idea of disorder, as we meet it in Locke, Addison, and Johnson, is highly relevant to the satire of the later seventeenth and early eighteenth centuries. To put this statement somewhat more pointedly, false judgment, mixed wit, and the discordia concors taken together define the idea of disorder which is the focus of attack in the satiric literature of the period. I think I can begin this inquiry by looking first at one specific source of imagery and some of the syntactical modes commonly employed in poetic satire and particularly in Pope's satires. My immediate purpose will be to show that the imagery and the syntax exploit the comedy of the discordia concors, and that various literary devices serve to build up a rhetorical foundation basic to the greater elaborations of folly within the satires. For example, we have recently been told that puns are Pope's "most prolific source of imagery in his comic and satiric poetry,"[12] and serve to yoke together the most violently heterogeneous ideas. In such an expression as "Or stain her honour, or her new brocade," it is apparent that the syntactical pressures of the line force upon the focal word, stain, the task of controlling two disparate meanings.[13] The two meanings are consequent upon using the literal and metaphorical meanings of a single verb to govern two objects. The meanings thus brought into equivalence through the action of the verb help define the milieu of absurd values that is under attack. Approximate to this sort of metaphorical effect is a curious use of rhyme in which phonetic likenesses are used to insinuate dissimilar or even opposite meanings. While the rhyme words are necessarily related by the logical structure of the couplet, their dissimilar meanings in phonetic relation also contribute to the comedy of the discordia concors. Take the equally familiar example: "Whether the nymph shall break Diana's law, / Or some frail China jar receive a flaw." The different and dissimilar denotative values of law and flaw reinforce the comedy of false relations. Such syntactical strategies as juxtaposition, parallelism, and antithesis provide continual possibilities for a witty duplicity of meaning and further explore the nature of disorder characterizing the satiric victim. The examples are so common not only in Pope's poetry but in the satire of the later seventeenth century that they may be chosen almost at random: From Dryden's The Medal: "So like the man, so golden to the sight, / So base within, so counterfeit and light"; from Mac Flecknoe: "A tun of man in thy large bulk is writ, / But sure thou'rt but a kilderkin of wit"; from the Epistle to a Lady: "Chaste to her husband, frank to all beside, / A teeming mistress, but a barren bride"; and from the Epistle to Dr. Arbuthnot: "Now high, now low, now master up, now miss, / And he himself one vile antithesis." These examples could be continued indefinitely; they present an idea of disorder that depends upon the union of incongruities, of antitheses meeting in the person, character, and intellect of the satiric victim.

Belinda, the heroine of The Rape of the Lock, is an excellent case in point, perhaps particularly as she is not vilified and her folly, however egregious, is not vicious. She offers a delightful example of folly consonant with the terms I have here brought together. After her rape she laments: "Oh hadst thou, cruel! been content to seize / Hairs less in sight, or any hairs but these." Her error is both profoundly witty (at her own expense of course) and profoundly immoral. She has, with some humorous justice however, found a likeness between one thing and another, but the foundations for such a likeness are laid, in Addison's terms, partly in falsehood and partly in truth. More severely is Atossa satirized by Pope in the Epistle to a Lady, and Pope makes rhetorical use of antitheses to define the yoked incongruities which distinguish her character. Perhaps, however, one of the most severely vilified figures in the poetic satire of the period is the Shaftesbury of Absalom and Achitophel. I introduce him here, along with Belinda and Atossa, to suggest that a rising acerbity in the attitudes of the satirist toward his subject, and a rising seriousness in the folly condemned, does not require a basic change in the terms of rebuke. Where Belinda is merely foolish, and Atossa vicious, Achitophel is evil. Dryden is unequivocal on the point. But evil does not force the satirist to change the terms in which folly is perceived, for evil is internal discord severely intensified. The change that does occur is in the tenor of the poem's levity. To state it very simply, Dryden is seldom, if ever, as amusing at Achitophel's expense as Pope can afford to be at Belinda's. And, moreover, Dryden is seldom as witty to Shaftesbury's cost in Absalom and Achitophel as he is with the same Shaftesbury in The Medal. To some extent, of course, wit is relevant to the satiric kind or genre; indecorous conceits are more appropriate to low satire than to high, to Hudibras, for example, than to Absalom and Achitophel. But my argument is not dependent upon the kinds of conceits employed to expose the satiric victim; on the contrary, my argument suggests only that whether the comedy be low or high, whether the satirist vilifies or rebukes, the related terms of failed judgment, mixed wit, and discordia concors will define the satiric victim and find rhetorical expression appropriate to the kind or genre.

But it may at this point be objected that Dr. Johnson used the term discordia concors both as a definition of, and as a protest against, the kind of poetry we normally associate with non-satiric literature, and that I am here perversely wrenching the term out of its historical and critical context. Indeed, we must keep in mind that Johnson was decrying the use of extravagant conceits not in satire, but in lyric poetry, and that for a poet to affect the metaphysics seemed to deny and pervert the expression of a typical feeling easily shared by others. That my use of the term is not anomalous, however, can be defended historically. The employment of the discordia concors to define the folly of the satiric victim may well be referred to Butler's Hudibras, a work which began to appear as early as 1663. Professor Jack has remarked that the "satirical tendency implicit in metaphysical poetry from the first is very marked in the work of Cleveland; in Butler, it might be said, this tendency becomes fully developed . . . . More brilliantly than any previous poet, he [Butler] used [metaphysical] 'wit' for the purposes of low satire . . . . Hudibras was one of the principal channels by which the 'wit' of the earlier part of the century was transmitted to the greatest of the Augustans."[14]

It may be useful here if we observe that one kind of approved wit in the later seventeenth century is akin to judgment. This is the meaning that Hobbes gives to the term wit in the Leviathan. As he says there, "Judgment . . . without fancy is wit, but fancy without judgment, not."[15] In effect, this rather limited meaning of wit introduces or reinforces a degree of caution in the use of wit in lyric poetry, and is obviously a definition arising from the reaction to metaphysical wit. But it is important to note that such a definition of approved or permissible wit opens the way for the different employment of metaphysical wit within the range of satire and for the purposes of excoriation.

The argument I have so far been proposing can be further developed. Beyond the particular examples of image, syntax, rhetorical strategy, and the follies of the satiric victim, we can consider another application of those related terms to the satire of the period. Through the critical use of such terms, and their adaptation to the purposes of satire, the later seventeenth and early eighteenth centuries were quite clearly developing a vocabulary to recognize and to stigmatize disorder. This is a point to which I shall have occasion to return. Beyond such examples, however, as those I have already offered, it seems useful at this time to enlarge our perspective and consider, even if briefly, the larger subject of genre. I have in mind particularly the mock heroic, important for the obvious reason of its resemblance to the heroic or epic poem. For the purposes of my argument it is useful to remark on the mock heroic as a mode in which the episodic pattern is clearly modelled on the comedy of low things taken to be high, and thus by juxtaposition deflating events or characters having only a mock serious importance. A simple and familiar example is presented by The Rape of the Lock where such allusions as the visit to the Cave of Spleen, the game of ombre, the adorning of Belinda, and above all the extensive machinery of Ariel and the Sylphs, provide an implicit standard of reference that is, in the deflation, ridiculous. This kind of situational satire extends the comedy of false resemblances and further enforces the idea of disorder which it is the purpose of the satirist to define. The deliberate inflation of the satiric victim, and the attribution of a mock heroic grandeur to his actions and to the situation in which he finds himself, suggest an elaboration of the disorder, and provide a method which the age found congenial to the purposes of satire. Moreover, the further application of methods of description familiar in classical literature to scenes of contemporary low life also enforces the comedy of false resemblances. Shadwell's coronation in Mac Flecknoe, for example, is heralded by enthusiastic cries from Pissing Alley, and offal floats along the water accompanying the vessel carrying the kingly dunce to his coronation. Such accompaniments are, in effect, appropriate tributes to his internal disorder, and the satirist's mock insistence upon the congruity of the high and the low sustains a relation that must at every point reveal the absurdities of Shadwell's situation. The more pervasive and culturally significant the false relations upon which the dunce insists, and by which he is characterized, the more the comedy darkens and moves from representing folly to proclaiming disaster. Such is the case in the closing passage of Dunciad IV, where Dulness comes forth to extinguish the arts of civilization, "and Universal Darkness buries All." Pope does not mean, in the figure of Dulness, to signify mere stupidity. Her descent from Chaos and eternal Night indicates rather something more important than slowness of comprehension. She is, as Warburton observed, "A ruling principle, not inert, but turning topsy-turvey the Understanding, and inducing an Anarchy or confused state of Mind."[16]

Warburton's statement defines the object of the satirist's attack and helps also to explain the varying intensities of satiric indictment as we move from one poem to another. As a general rule, attack varies in intensity according to the extent to which the satiric victim menaces the security of a just and appropriate order. Thus, Achitophel is a more serious threat to the order of a civilization than is Belinda, Sporus more so than Atossa. Generally, also, the satirist at least by implication states the case for conservative rather than innovative values. Moreover, he imposes upon us the necessity of seeing the object of attack from a singularly limited perspective. This fact may help explain one of the peculiar effects of satire that most readers have probably noticed. Satire diminishes the victim quite in proportion to the way it elevates the intelligence controlling the poem. In other words, the satiric victim and the author behind the poem are often further apart empathically than in any other form of literature. I suspect that the distance between the two is explicable in terms of the relation between the failed judgment of the victim and the true wit of the satirist. This is to say that the means by which the judgment of the victim is revealed as inadequate necessitates the exercise of the satirist's triumphant wit. The more the latter can delight and surprise us, the more he must inevitably depress the judgment of the former. As the one goes up the other goes down. The statement provides us with a position from which we can look briefly at the fourth book of Gulliver's Travels.

We know that in this work Gulliver is bewildered by the Yahoos, who seem to him unfortunately like mankind. We know also that Gulliver admires the Houyhnhnms, who seem to him better than mankind, but what man might be if he made the best of his faculties. Clearly, Gulliver's attitudes create problems for us, simply because, as Martin Price remarks, Swift is "demanding of his readers what he never grants to Gulliver, the power to make necessary distinctions." Moreover, "Gulliver fails to make the most important distinction of all -- between animal rationale and animal rationis capax."[17] The distinction takes us back to Locke's comment on judgment, and reminds us that inadequate judgment results in the false likenings of the discordia concors. The Yahoos are taken by Gulliver to be a likeness of what man is, while the Houyhnhnms are taken to be a likeness of what man should be. And both likenings are false. Dr. Johnson said of *Gulliver's Travels* that once you have thought of the idea of big and little men the rest was inevitable. Dr. Johnson, I think, has it just backwards. Once you have introduced the comedy of true and false likenings, it follows that you may very well use the relativistic devices that Swift employs to advance the comedy. So, then, does the human body in Brobdingnag become monstrous when viewed with the microscopic eye, but the Brobdingnagians are not men, and man's eye is not microscopic when applied to his own kind. To employ the standards of human life in an inverted relationship is to draw false likenesses. It is to say, in effect, that this is what man's body is like, that this is the real fact of human beauty, when of course it is nothing of the sort. Over and again Gulliver is betrayed by seeming likenesses, but likenesses that depend for their veracity upon perverting the real nature of the human condition. But so also is Gulliver confronted by true likenesses to man, likenesses that are disguised in unlikenesses. And finally we realize the exact nature of the perilous quest on which Swift has sent him: it is nothing less than to discover who and what man is. In the brilliant game of analogies Gulliver finally loses his way and sinks into madness, perplexed by the resemblances to man of creatures who are apparently unlike him, perplexed equally by resemblances which are laid, in Addison's terms, partly in truth and partly in falsehood.

The true aspirant to Dulness, Pope tells us in *Peri Bathous*, "mingle[s] bits of the most various or discordant kinds . . . and connect[s] them . . . by heads or by tails, as it shall please his imagination."[18] Such, I have been arguing, is the essential characteristic of the satiric victim guilty of false ideas of order, ideas having their foundation in inadequate discrimination and in the inappropriateness of false resemblances. Now there is implicit in this condition a relation between the satiric victim and the tragic hero that is worth pursuing. The mind of the satiric victim is confused in a manner suitable to the true aspirant to dullness, but the mind of the tragic hero is perplexed by incongruities that he too seeks to reconcile and bring into order. That is, the tragic hero cannot reconcile those internal oppositions which his greatness has caused to arise; the satiric victim, on the other hand, cannot refrain from making false likenings which his folly has brought upon him. I should like to probe this subject a bit in the hope of relating one characteristic attitude toward tragedy in the later seventeenth century to the idea of disorder that I have been so far setting out. Allardyce Nicoll has remarked, speaking of early eighteenth-century English drama, that "Tragedy as a whole is clearly subordinate in the repertoires, in the early years to comedy, later to opera and comedy, and towards the middle and end of the period, to opera, comedy, and pantomime."[19] And here I should like to place this fact in relation to another. In 1680 Nahum Tate unhappily revised King Lear so as to permit a happy ending. Lear is in Tate's version restored to the throne and Cordelia is married to Edgar. There is a great deal of nonsense in Tate's revision not worth pausing over, but one consideration in particular is pertinent to my argument. In rewriting the play, Tate wished not only "to rectify what was wanting in the regularity and probability of the tale"; beyond such alterations he both modified and limited the turmoil of Lear's mind in which the discordances of his thought provide the basis for the grandeur of his madness.[20] Let us remember that Tate's alteration of the play held the stage for a century and a half. Betterton acted Tate's version, Garrick acted it, and Dr. Johnson approved it. The popularity of Tate's desecration is related not only, I think, to the pathetic distress of the lovers, characteristic of the Restoration heroic drama, and not only to Dr. Johnson's preference for "the final triumph of persecuted virtue."[21] Beyond such appeals, Tate's revision reduced the discord raging within Lear's mind; mitigated, that is, the mental chaos which neoclassic rationality was more apt to regard as distinctive of the satiric victim rather than the tragic hero.

In much the same way does Dryden debilitate Antony's tragic greatness, making him, rather, into the pawn of various conspiratorial forces so that he is both more pathetic and less complexly constituted. Alterations and adaptations of this sort were, as we know, fairly commonplace. They frequently delimited the range and scope of action and tended to oversimplify character. Tate's explanation is perhaps not uncharacteristic of the motives governing the adapters: "I found the whole," he says of Lear, "a heap of jewels, unstrung and unpolished; yet so dazzling in their disorder, that I soon perceived I had seized a treasure."[22] "So dazzling in their disorder"; the phrase takes us back to the cosmos of disorder and to the satirist's triumphant creation of it.

Let me at this point recall the argument to its original purposes. I have intended to suggest a relation among several critical terms, and I have proposed that these terms can be used to orient ourselves to many satires of the later seventeenth and early eighteenth centuries. Locke's definition of judgment, Addison's of mixed wit, and Johnson's of the discordia concors suggest to me a highly scrupulous and sustained attention to a common idea of disorder. The importance of these terms, their authoritative centrality, so to speak, may also suggest something else of value about the periods I am touching upon here. A highly critical awareness of the source and origin of disorder implies a certain narrowing of possibility, a certain tendency toward a radical impermissiveness in the making of new ideas of order. What I wish to suggest in a purely speculative spirit I shall at least be definite about. The legacy of Augustan satire, and of the values inherent within it, was a distrust of intellectual innovation, of innovation based upon the union of radically dissimilar parts. Disorder for such as Locke, Addison and Johnson was a condition in which the judgment has failed to play its proper role, and the consequences were evident in satires attacking relationships both false and potentially disastrous. The Augustan satirist had found a pattern for recognizing the fallacious and the vicious; or, more exactly, he had reduced the fallacious and the vicious to a pattern. The idea of disorder restricted the possibility for new patterns of order, if only because order was predicated upon the belief that things dissimilar are things disparate, unsusceptible to reconciliation or to synthesis. The delimitations fostered by the idea of disorder that I have set out here fell in with other ideas, if so they may be called, current in the period: with, for instance, the social ethic of adaptation as a principle ruling the relation between individual and society (Tom Jones is an excellent example); with the doctrine of uniformitarianism, of exemplary importance in English thought from Bolingbroke and Pope to Reynolds and Johnson; with an idea of history emphasizing historical movement as a predictable dynamism, an idea patent in The Vanity of Human Wishes and the Elegy Written in a Country Church-yard; and with the empirically derived and normative functions of associationism. All such ideas either obviated or seriously limited the radically different and unique, and all such served a philosophy of human limitation which lies heavily over the literature of the later eighteenth century.

Such statements to be sure require justification, indeed a good deal of justification, which I beg offering here and now. Principally, however, a symbolic literature of the kind we normally associate with English Romantic poetry requires that divergent or seemingly incompatible meanings be imposed upon a subject, and that these meanings function interrelatedly with one another to build up complex structures. Frye points out that such "a technique of symbolism . . . is based on a strong sense of a lurking antagonism between the literal and the descriptive aspects of symbols."[23] These antagonisms grow and expand into something complex because they do not cancel each other out but develop meanings accretively. Romantic literature is filled with examples where the object is perceived so diversely that any specific meaning it might have, any literal meaning, is overlaid by a profusion of related meanings.

As I have partially indicated, Augustan satire, particularly in the hands of such masters as Swift or Pope, could present a brilliant and bewildering diversity of meanings, or of situational possibilities and moral values, but normally the implication remains that one meaning is right and true, the others chimeras to be judiciously differentiated from the one that is unexceptionable. Taken together these remarks indicate why Romantic literature is radically permissive, granting indulgence to esoteric or aberrant states of mind. Such states of mind are necessary for the emergence of new awarenesses that deepen and extend the complexity of the object perceived as symbol. Just the opposite is normally true of Augustan literature, which embodies attitudes highly suspicious of such states of mind and which discourages those eccentricities of thought or feeling that interfere with the sober discriminations of the judgment. Here is one of the reasons why enthusiasm was proscribed in the name of rationality.

But it is plain that my subject is now taking me in a variety of different directions, in none of which I wish to go. The thesis of the paper has been, I hope, sufficiently clear not to require restatement. That much Augustan satire was related to the terms I have introduced here has also, I believe, been made apparent. That a compelling idea of disorder was bequeathed to the later eighteenth century and that the vitality of this idea limited the range and power of the literature, particularly its lyric and dramatic forms, remains to be proved. I trust that I shall have a later occasion to do so.

Duke University

## NOTES

1. *Lives of the English Poets* (London, 1941), I, 11.

2. *An Essay on Man*, ed. Maynard Mack (London, 1950), p. xxxiv.

3. *Characteristics*, ed. J.M. Robertson (Gloucester, Mass., 1963), II, 22.

4. Earl Wasserman, *The Subtler Language* (Baltimore, 1959), p. 176.

5. *Ibid.*, p. 177.

6. Mack, p. liv.

7. *Ibid.*, p. liv-lv.

8. *The Great Chain of Being* (New York, 1960), pp. 65-66.

9. Wasserman, pp. 178-79.

10. *Essay*, ed. A.C. Fraser (New York, 1959), I, 203.

11. *Eighteenth-Century Critical Essays*, ed. Scott Elledge (Ithaca, N.Y., 1961), I, 15.

12. Maynard Mack, "'Wit and Poetry and Pope': Some Observations on his Imagery," *Eighteenth Century English Literature*, ed. James L. Clifford (New York, 1959), p. 31.

13. *Alexander Pope, Selected Poetry and Prose*, ed. W.K. Wimsatt (New York, 1951), p. xxx.

14. Ian Jack, *Augustan Satire* (Oxford, 1952), pp. 35-36.

15. *Hobbes, Selections*, ed. F.J.E. Woodbridge (New York, 1958), p. 221.

16. Jack, p. 124.

17. *To the Palace of Wisdom* (New York, 1964), p. 199.

18. *Peri Bathous*, ch. v.

19. *A History of English Drama* (Cambridge, 1961), II, 59.

20. Moody E. Prior, <u>The Language of Tragedy</u> (Bloomington, Ind., 1966), p. 181.

21. <u>Ibid.</u>, p. 180.

22. <u>Ibid.</u>, p. 181.

23. <u>Anatomy of Criticism</u> (Princeton, 1957), p. 92.

THE SCHEDULED QUEST*

By Carey McIntosh

I am assuming that the word "Augustan" identifies not only a period, $x$ number of years, but also a distinctive set of attitudes; that during the seventeenth and eighteenth centuries some writers are more Augustan than others, and some genres more characteristic than others of the Augustan temper.

It is not possible to talk meaningfully about Augustan genres without abandoning prejudices against didacticism, or unless we understand that in some of the best of English literature didactic and aesthetic forces work not at cross-purposes but in harmony. This I think is a key to analysis and appreciation of Augustan genres, a recognition of the profound moralism of the Augustan mind, and of the delight Augustan writers took in instruction. For this reason the traditional tripartite division of genres into epic, lyric, and dramatic simply is not large enough to handle eighteenth-century literature; and Augustan theorists, preoccupied with decorum, with the consequences of a given genre's position on the social, psychological, and stylistic hierarchy, seem frequently irrelevant to literary practice of the time.

An awareness of the power of didacticism helps us understand why formal epic sickened and died in our period, and why, in Johnson's words, "Crush'd by rules, and weaken'd as refin'd, / For years the power of tragedy declined." Beowulf is worthy of epic because, like the mountain, he is there, not because he embodies the values of the comitatus or Christianized paganism; and the moral value that any tragedy implies is a relatively minor aspect of its impact as tragedy. On the other hand, didactic, critical genres flourished between 1660 and 1776, satire in particular, but also satirical comedy, comedy of manners, satirical-comical novel of manners, burlesque, georgic, epistle, essay.

---

\* Since space was severely limited, I restricted myself to <u>one</u> aspect of generic practice (not theory), and to <u>one</u> example. Such cursory treatment is regrettable; I hope to atone for it in the not too distant future by expanding at least the second part of this essay to its proper dimensions.

Degree of didacticism helps distinguish between more Augustan genres and less Augustan genres: satire is more Augustan than the greater ode, and the "Pindarick madness" that produced these greater odes smouldered under the surface between Congreve and Gray, more or less ignored by major poets during the reign of the Scriblerians. Degree of didacticism also helps distinguish between authors who are more Augustan or less Augustan. Swift is more Augustan than Pope because his soul never melts in mournful lays, as Pope's does in addressing the Unfortunate Lady; Addison more Augustan than Steele because less subject to personal enthusiasms. Johnson contemplates death in the <u>Rambler</u> as an instrument of moral discipline -- which makes him more Augustan than the graveyard poets, who contemplate death as often for the "pleasures of melancholy" as for self-improvement.

The survey, or "scheduled quest," is an interesting example of an Augustan petit-genre or generic principle that answered didactic needs. The impulse to survey mankind from China to Peru is a universal one, but it is chiefly in the eighteenth century that didactic surveys blossom tremendously into literature. The Augustan survey is not truly scholarly (as the perfect Baconian collection would be), but borrows some of the procedures of scholarly inquiry: it is not an avenue to truth so much as a means of displaying a truth. It is an anthology, not a complete bibliography, and anthologies require a point of view.

Extended into the realm of ideas, the Augustan survey ranges swiftly through the larger categories of ethics or philosophy in order to come to a conclusion that has in fact already been arrived at, a conclusion often announced in the opening lines. Thus, <u>Religio Laici</u>, Prior's <u>Solomon</u>, <u>The Vanity of Human Wishes</u>, <u>Rasselas</u> -- each of these is organized tightly or loosely as a <u>catalogue raisonnée</u> designed to instruct as well as entertain.

Extended in space, the Augustan survey makes a philosophic journey, like <u>Gulliver's Travels</u>, or like Goldsmith's <u>Traveller</u>, or Matthew Bramble's <u>Expedition</u>, or like the Man of the Hill's tiny tour of Europe in <u>Tom Jones</u>.

Extended in time, the Augustan survey deals in capsule histories and in the miniature biographies so common in the periodical essays; in the adventures of a guinea, in a rake's progress.

Less didactic and "scheduled" surveys are by that very fact less Augustan: "progress poetry" as in Gray and Collins is in essence celebratory; the Club that became a fixture of periodical essays after 1711 is meant to extend the range of the author-editor into all the principal branches of society, from cit to squire to beau, but its didacticism is perceptibly diluted by simple pleasure in variety of point of view. The Excursion Poetry of James Thomson surveys nature primarily to praise the God of nature: first description, then sermon.

But all Augustan surveys have a good idea either of where they are going or where they stand. The Spectator, detached and evaluating, gave way later in the century to the Wanderer, bemused but sensitive -- Romantic quests are essentially uncertain about what they are looking for: the poet of Alastor, in his own words, "left / His cold friends and alienated home / To seek strange truths in undiscovered lands."

University of Rochester

1968 NEOCLASSICISM SEMINAR

SEMINAR 64: PROBLEMS OF NEOCLASSICISM: THEORIES OF IMITATION

Discussion leader, PAUL J. KORSHIN, Univ. of Pennsylvania

Sunday, 29 December 1968, 1:15-2:30 P.M.

I. Introductory statement (5 minutes)

II. Brief comments on papers (25 minutes).
    Each panelist will discuss, not read, his paper.

   1. Leon M. Guilhamet, Yale Univ., "Imitation and Originality in the Poems of Thomas Gray." Pages 1-23 of the collected papers sent to participants, and available at the meeting.

   2. Howard D. Weinbrot, Univ. of Wisconsin, "Augustan Imitation: The Role of the Original." Pages 24-51 of the collected papers.

   3. Jeffrey Hart, Dartmouth College, "Particular and General Truth: Some Speculative Footnotes to Scott Elledge." Pages 52-68 of the collected papers.

   4. Harvey D. Goldstein, Univ. of Southern California, "The Epistemological Basis of Eighteenth-Century Theories of Imitation."
      Professor Goldstein's paper was unavailable for distribution in advance of the meeting.

III. Questions and discussion (45 minutes)

# IMITATION AND ORIGINALITY IN THE POEMS OF THOMAS GRAY

By Leon M. Guilhamet

I propose to consider the problem of imitation and originality in Gray's poems from a fairly simple perspective, that provided by Plato in Book III of the Republic.

It will be recalled that Socrates defines "everything that's said by tellers of tales or poets..." as "a narrative of what has come to pass, what is, or what is going to be ...."[1] Narration (diēgēsis) is then divided into three categories: simple narration, imitation, and a union of the two. Gray's own notes summarize Plato's position:

> Poetick eloquence is divided into narration (in the writer's own person), and imitation (in some assumed character). Dithyrambicks usually consist wholly of the former, dramatick poesy of the latter, the epick, &c. of both mixed.[2]

As Gray's note indicates, the question as to whether or not a work is imitative depends solely on our analysis of the speaker's voice. If the poet speaks in his own voice, the poem is pure narrative; if he employs a persona, the work is imitative.

Nearly twenty years after the death of Gray, Thomas Twining, the estimable editor of Aristotle, reluctantly admitted the relevance of imitation as applied to description, fiction, and sound, but preferred to limit its use to a dramatic meaning:

> There seems to be but _one_ view in which Poetry can be considered as _Imitation_, in the strict and proper sense of the word. If we look for both _immediate_ and _obvious_ resemblance, we shall find it only in _dramatic_ -- or to use a more general term -- _personative_ Poetry; that is, all Poetry in which, whether essentially or occasionally, the Poet personates; for here, _speech_ is imitated by speech.[3]

Twining mentions only tragedy, comedy, and epic among literary genres as "personative." Gray's odes, presumably, under the Platonic formula, would be pure narrative, with The Bard a clear exception. Indeed, that poem is ostensibly dithyrambic, but the main speaker is the "personated" Welsh bard. There is, of course, another speaker in the poem, suggesting that it is, like epic, a mixture of imitation and narrative.

Though Gray is never very specific or helpful on the concept of imitation, it is likely that his understanding of it was more comprehensive (and confused) than Twining's. Though he knew and used the limited Platonic conception, he seems unpedantic on this point. He readily accepts the usual notion of imitation of style, both of ancient and modern authors, and it is reasonably certain that he knew some of the modern conceptions of imitation, if only through his friend Richard Hurd's A Discourse on Poetical Imitation and the supplementary A Dissertation on the Marks of Imitation.[4]

In Hurd's work the concept of imitation is far from the neoclassical pictorialism of Horace's ut pictura poesis. Hurd has a high regard for what he calls "painting in poetry," but "the most sublime and interesting of all the modes of imitation" is the imitation of mental processes.[5] "Painting...," he writes, "can express the material universe, and, as will be seen hereafter, can evidence the internal movements of the soul by sensible marks and symbols: but it is poetry alone, which delineates the mind itself, and opens the recesses of the heart to us."[6]

For Hurd imitation at a certain level includes originality:

> The objects of imitation, like the materials of human knowledge, are a common stock, which experience furnishes to all men. And it is in the operations of the mind upon them, that the glory of poetry, as of science, consists. Here the genius of the poet hath room to shew itself; and from hence alone is the praise of originality to be ascertained.[7]

This concern for mind on Hurd's part agrees well enough with Plato's concern for the narrative or imitative voice of the poet. Neither Hurd nor Plato emphasizes the materials of imitation, but rather the process and results of the imitative act.

When Hurd mentions the materials of imitation, he means not only Nature in all its complexity, but also the works of other authors. As might be expected, slavish, inferior imitation is denounced, but Hurd is careful to show that some apparent imitation is really originality:

> Common sense directs us, for the most part, to regard resemblances in great writers, not as the pilferings, or frugal acquisitions of needy art, but as the honest fruits of genius, the free and liberal beauties of unenvying nature.[8]

This would seem to cover Gray's borrowings with the cloak of genius. "The expression of two writers," Hurd writes," may be similar, and sometimes even identical, and yet be original in both."[9] And later in his study, as Hurd warms to his subject, he suggests that imitators require even more invention than do originals.[10] But this is in imitation of the highest kind.

This conscious confusion of original composition and imitation can be seen in Edward Young as well:

> The mind of a man of genius is a fertile and pleasant field, pleasant as Elysium, and fertile as Tempe; it enjoys a perpetual spring. Of that spring, Originals are the fairest flowers: Imitations are of quicker growth, but fainter bloom. Imitations are of two kinds; one of nature, one of authors: The first we call Originals, and confine the term Imitation to the second.[11]

There were, to be sure, those who denied that poetry was imitative art, such as Edmund Burke and, later in the century, Sir William Jones; but these were relatively few. In short, imitation was an article of faith at mid-century, but since each author defines it as he will, it had little value as a critical term.

There is reason to believe that Gray's concept of imitation was more scholarly, closer to the Greek sources than that of most of his contemporaries. We know that he undertook a careful study of Aristotle, including the Poetics, during 1746. His extensive notes on Plato prove that he knew the Platonic position on imitation and art in general.

This intimate acquaintance with the sources themselves is characteristic of Gray's approach to any subject, whether poetry, philosophy, or botany. Since he trusted his own ability to understand ancient or modern texts without the help of commentary, he read relatively little contemporary criticism, and thus seems to have been uninfluenced by specific critical trends. He did read widely in modern poetry, however, which accounts in part for the contemporaneity of technique and theme in his own poetry.

Indeed, this characteristic independence and first-hand acquaintance with the classics give Gray's poetry and thought a clarity and good sense lacking in most of his contemporaries. His vast knowledge and acute understanding of the classical authors prevented him from underestimating them and from being taken in by the false glitter of newfangled ideas. His editor T.J. Mathias, in lavishly praising Gray's classical sensitivity, makes clear that he "revolted from the vapid, vague, and unmeaning effusions of writers who, refusing to submit to the indispensable laws of lyrical poetry, or from ignorance of them, called their own wildness, genius, and their contempt of rules, originality."[12]

Certainly these sentiments may be properly applied to Gray, but they do not tell the whole story. Gray was greatly attracted to the concept of originality. For example, when Goldsmith, greatly admiring Gray's odes, wrote in The Monthly Review that "instead of being an imitator," he should venture "to be more original," Gray could single out that specific advice for praise:

> The Review I have read, & admire it, particularly that observation that the Bard is taken from Pastor cum traheret, & the advice to be more an original, & in order to be so, the way is (he says) to cultivate the native flowers of the soil, & not introduce the exoticks of another climate.[13]

Some comments on poetic inspiration in a letter to Wharton further reflect the complexity of Gray's view of poetry:

> I by no means pretend to inspiration, but yet I affirm, that the faculty in question is by no means voluntary. It is the result (I suppose) of a certain disposition of mind, w$^{ch}$ does not depend on oneself, & w$^{ch}$ I have not felt this long time. You that are a witness, how seldom this spirit has moved me in my life, may easily give credit to what I say.[14]

Here is the dispassionate Gray somewhere between pure spontaneity and labored craft. "You apprehend too much from my resolutions about writing...," he wrote to Wharton some six months earlier, "they are only made to be broken, & after all it will be just as the maggot bites."[15] And fairly late in his life Gray was to criticize the notion that certain thoughts and expressions were suitable to only one species of poetry: "Rules are but chains, good for little, except when one can break through them; and what is fine gives me so much pleasure, that I never regard what place it is in."[16]

The problem of choosing between learned imitation and originality was a serious one for Gray. He comments on the most recent volumes of the Dodsley Collection:

> particularly Dr. Akenside is in a deplorable way. What signifies Learning and the Ancients, (Mason will say triumphantly) why should people read Greek to lose their imagination, their ear, and their mother tongue? But then there is Mr. Shenstone, who trusts to nature and simple sentiment, why does he do no better? he goes hopping along his own gravel-walks, and never deviates from the beaten paths for fear of being lost.[17]

The simple and pretty style of Shenstone will not do; loftiness can be gained, it seemed to Gray, only through imitation; and yet imitation could go far wrong too, as in the poetry of Akenside. Of course Shenstone is an imitator too, whether of Spenser or Tibullus, a fact which Gray must have recognized. Goldsmith's call for a simpler, characteristically more English style had, it seemed, been heeded by Shenstone, and the results were unsatisfactory.

Yet Gray, in recognizing the deficiencies of Shenstone, may have realized the implications of this call to a simple style. It was a call not only to put aside the neo-classical ideas of separate genres, but an exhortation to the poet to reject the mimic art of many voices and begin the search for one, the poet's very own voice.

Shenstone's part in this movement may be suggested by some lines from his first Elegy:

> Ne'er may my vintage glad the sordid breast;
> Ne'er tinge the lip that dares be unsincere.
>
> . . . . . . . . . . . . . . . . . . . . . . . . . . .
>
> Far from these paths, ye faithless friends, depart!
> Fly my plain board, abhor my hostile name!
> Hence! the faint verse that flows not from the heart,
> But mourns in labour'd strains, the price of fame.
>
> . . . . . . . . . . . . . . . . . . . . . . . . . . .
>
> Write from thy bosom -- let not art controul
> The ready pen, that makes his edicts known.

The trouble with Shenstone is not, as Gray indicated, that he trusts to nature and simple sentiment -- though it is possible for simple sentiment to be all too simple. The trouble is that in trying to write from his own heart -- to discover his own voice -- he continues to sound like everyone else, alternately, confusedly, and finally, as Jonson thought wrongly of Spenser, he writes no language. The appropriation of other authors does not necessarily result in richness of poetic composition, especially when the intention is, presumably, to write sincerely from the heart.

To illustrate this more clearly, we should return to Plato's
Republic. Plato, as will be recalled, distinguishes between narration (diēgēsis) and imitation (mimēsis) in that the first is in
the poet's own voice, while imitation is personation. Thus according to Plato narration

> involves only small changes, and, if someone assigns the appropriate
> harmonic mode and rhythm to the style, it turns out that the man
> who speaks correctly speaks mostly in the same style and in one
> mode, for the changes are small, and likewise in a similar rhythm.[18]

In other words there is a sameness of voice in style, inflection,
and so on -- readily identifiable as belonging to one man; for in
Plato's Republic, "there's no double man among us, nor a manifold
one, since each man does one thing."[19] But imitation, on the other
hand, requires "all modes and all rhythms -- if it's going to speak
in its own way, because it involves all species of changes...."[20]

Just as a dramatist must have a voice for every character in his
play, the classical author must have a voice appropriate to every
genre he determines to work in. Edward Young, for example, imitates
Dryden in his early heroic verse; and in his plays attempts to
imitate Shakespeare. Love of Fame, as Howard D. Weinbrot has shown,
reveals a tension between genteel mask and apocalypse, resulting
in serious internal contradictions.[21] The Night Thoughts comes
closest to being a conscious attempt to find his own voice, but
he cannot liberate the blank verse line from imitation of Milton.

Collins, too, may be said to follow this pattern. From his curious
Persian Eclogues, he progresses through a learned classical style,
concluding his career with "An Ode on the Popular Superstitions of
the Highlands of Scotland," using native British material, as Goldsmith was to advise Gray in 1757. Perhaps Collins was on his way
to finding his own poetic voice.

The struggle to find the single voice appropriate to all poetry
can be seen more readily perhaps in Wordsworth's labors through
"An Evening Walk" and "Descriptive Sketches," and even through
the dull simplicity of many poems in Lyrical Ballads. But with
"Tintern Abbey", parts of The Excursion, and The Prelude, we hear
the single, purportedly sincere, and recognizable voice of Wordsworth. Here is blank verse freed of imitation, except in some few
humorless parodies in which Wordsworth seemingly exorcises his
powers of imitation.

Much the same pattern can be seen in Keats as he works out of early imitations of Spenser and Leigh Hunt, through imitation of Milton in Hyperion, imitation of Shakespeare in Otho the Great and King Stephen, to the distinct and inimitable voice of the Great Odes and The Fall of Hyperion. In this last-mentioned poem, Keats frees his blank verse line from both Miltonic and Wordsworthian dependence.[22]

In a paper recently delivered at the English Institute, Professor W.K. Wimsatt has warned against the assumption that imitation inevitably means servility, and revolution, whether in politics or poetry, leads to freedom.[23] By showing the possible variety within imitative modes, he suggests that the reverse may be true. Indeed, "originality" or uniqueness, for all its positive connotation, suggests singleness and limitation. Many forms of imitation, on the other hand, require a special act of imagination. Gray seems to have agreed. In his essay on Samuel Daniel, he wrote that elegy

> requires no other order or invention than those of pure, simple nature, what is (or what ought to appear) the result of a feeling mind strongly possess'd by its subject, and surely he that is so in poetry has done more than half his work, but it is not every imagination that can throw itself into all the situations of a fictitious subject.[24]

The conflict between the claims of originality and imitation in Gray's poetry has been expressed in different terms in two recent studies of Gray. Mr. F. Doherty in his essay "The Two Voices of Gray" distinguishes a public voice and a private voice. For Mr. Doherty "the characteristics of the public poetry are Gray's scholarly regard for accuracy, occurring as the 'translation' of prose fact into verse, and Gray's habitual desire to escape commonness . . . ."[25] This for Doherty represents Gray's imitative side, but more important is the personal, private aspect. Mr. Doherty writes:

> What seems quite plain to me is that he was more truly himself in those poems which are most loved and best known, because it is here that we hear the distinctive voice of Gray, depressed and shaded, expressing its gentle and gentlemanly sadness in a tone unique and recognisable.[26]

In a perceptive essay Bertrand Bronson also notices in Gray, this time in the Elegy, an "individual and even personal style and diction."[27] Professor Bronson assumes on Gray's part "personal involvement" and "the poem's inescapable egocentricity."[28] "The immediate, crucial difficulty," he writes,"is how to devise a memorial in the form of inscriptional verses for oneself that shall

be perfectly serious and emotionally sincere; that shall be neither
objectionably self-abasing nor apparently self-satisified; neither
too cold and impersonal to communicate emotion nor too revealing of
private emotion or self-commiseration."[29]   Bronson goes on ingeniously
to show how a "special decorum" achieves a balance between self-
revelation and neo-classical restraint.

In doing this Professor Bronson has provided not only a helpful
reading of the *Elegy*, but a truth to be pondered in a consideration
of Gray's other poems.  Clearly there is a tension in Gray between
the personal and the impersonal, whether in motif or diction, form
or style:  in short, between subjective expression and objective
imitation.  Let us turn to the poems themselves and see how this
tension operates.

In the "Ode on the Spring" the general application of theme is in
tension with the poet's self, though here the self is kept in
strict subordination to the thematic concern.  Thus in the second
stanza, where the poet's self is introduced

>           Beside some water's rushy brink
>           With me the Muse shall sit, and think
>           (At ease reclin'd in rustic state)[30]
>                           (15-17)

the poetry is shared with the personified Muse and the stanza hurries
on to general truths:

>           How vain the ardour of the Crowd,
>           How low, how little are the Proud,
>           How indigent the Great! (18-20)

The third and fourth stanzas by recourse to insect imagery appropriate
to the season illustrate how truly vain is the ardour of the crowd:

>           Yet hark, how thro' the peopled air
>           The busy murmur glows!
>           The insect youth are on the wing,
>           Eager to taste the honied spring, . . . (23-26)

The moralist poet then draws the moral in stanza four.  One is tempted
to see this obvious moralizing as a blemish -- after all the "insect
youth" of stanza three are not merely insects, but youths as well.

The application of the images of spring to man's life is already graphically explicit. But this would not be sufficient to Gray's purpose. The somewhat tedious moralizing of stanza four is drawn to characterize the poet; so that the unanticipated irony of stanza five can be brought home with perfect point: "Poor moralist! and what art thou? / A solitary fly!" (43-44). The poet has indeed been a moralist and of the worst kind, one without self-knowledge. The "sportive kind" of line 42 do not succeed in turning from their breast the sharp point of the poet's criticism, but they do succeed in implicating him in the general insufficiency of man. His life is by no means a good alternative to theirs; but enough irony turns against them in their reply to keep us from preferring their life, sunny and breezy though it be, to the shaded repose of the moralist poet.

Gray here succeeds in balancing perspectives in such a way that the voice of the poet never becomes the final arbiter. The poet's insufficiency renders him an object of scrutiny on the part of the reader, and this does not permit him to assume the role of authority and control which the voice in an ode normally possesses.

This tendency to undercut or at least balance the personal voice by shifting perspectives is characteristic of many of Gray's poems, suggesting that the attempt to speak in his own voice (if that is what it is) is unsuccessful. This lack of success may account for Gray's increasing tendency to turn to more strictly imitative styles in later poems.

In the "Ode on a Distant Prospect of Eton College" much the same pattern is discernible. The speaker notes the passion, poverty, sickness, and death which await the little boys of the college, reaching his high point of moral understanding in the final stanza:

>     To each his suff'rings: all are men,
>  Condemn'd alike to groan,
>  The tender for another's pain;
>  Th'unfeeling for his own. (91-94)

Here the speaker tempers his own wisdom with the full sympathy he seems to claim for himself. But perhaps this tender sympathy leads him to question the value of the "wisdom" which the poem has sought to express; sympathy leads to the desire to withhold the truth of the human situation from the playing children:

> Yet ah! why should they know their fate?
> Since sorrow never comes too late,
> And happiness too swiftly flies.
> Thought would destroy their paradise.
> No more; where ignorance is bliss,
> 'Tis folly to be wise. (95-100)

Though it is clear that the children will, as men, learn their fate, there is a desire on the speaker's part to withhold it from them -- perhaps even in adulthood -- if that were possible. The melancholy view of man articulated earlier in the poem is in these last lines revealed as too painful for contemplation, thereby undercutting the poet-moralist's position, as was done in the "Ode on the Spring." The poet cuts himself off abruptly: "No more," *basta*: "where ignorance is bliss, / 'Tis folly to be wise." The irony in these lines, directed against those who prefer ignorance and bliss, is not sufficient to make us reject the truth of the poet's insight into his own blunder and inadequacy. He is the one who consciously destroys paradise. He it is who has brought anger, fear, and shame before our eyes -- insisting that we accept them as our ineluctable fate.

By questioning the value of his own earlier observations, Gray once again creates distance between the speaker and the point of view derived from the poem, leaving us to wonder which point of view to accept, if any. By undercutting the earlier moralistic exposition, the voice of the poet is left curiously wavering.

Though a long list of sources for the two preceding poems could be given, the echoes which scholars have discovered in <u>The Progress of Poesy</u> are exceptionally remarkable in their number.[31] The poem is, of course, a Pindaric ode, and so Pindar is the essential object of imitation, but Mitford annotates the poem with references to more than thirty other authors. Certainly many, if not most, of the poem's possible echoes are questionable or clearly specious. Yet if only a fraction of them were relevant to the poem, the imitative quality of Gray's imagination would be hard to deny. Indeed, after our Pindaric flight, though we may believe we hear the poet's own voice at the end of the poem, the posture of poetic grandeur is Pindar's:

> Oh! Lyre divine, what daring Spirit
> Wakes thee now? tho' he inherit
> Nor the pride, nor ample pinion
> That the Theban Eagle bear
> Sailing with supreme dominion
> Thro' the azure deep of air . . . . (112-17)

Though the latest editors of Gray's poems, Starr and Hendrickson, assure us that the "daring Spirit" is Gray himself, it is entirely possible that he had his friend Mason in mind. The conclusion of Gray's previous note makes this a possibility: "Mr. Mason indeed of late days has touched the true chords, and with a masterly hand, in some of his Choruses -- above all in the last of Caractacus...."[32] But whether this is true or not, the result is one of ambiguity, of distancing the speaker from what he is saying. Far from being invited to assume that the poet is speaking in his own voice, it is made clear to us that the voice is, in part at least, that of another and that what is being said has several possible meanings.

Geoffrey Tillotson has noted the essentially dramatic structure of the "Sonnet on the Death of Richard West": "When Gray begins his poem with

> In vain to me the smileing Mornings shine,
>     And redning Phoebus lifts his golden Fire:
> The Birds in vain their amorous Descant joyn;
>     Or cheerful Fields resume their green Attire;
> These Ears, alas! for other Notes repine . . .

he means us to take the 'poetic diction' as dramatic -- for though it is himself who is speaking, he speaks by means of quotations from others."[33] These lines, cited by Tillotson, are juxtaposed with the diction of real grief: "I fruitless mourn to him, that cannot hear, / and weep the more because I weep in vain."

This early poem is something of an exemplum of Gray's struggle to assume his own voice. Though five of the six "personal" lines received the approbation of Wordsworth for their purer diction, it is important to note that the personal effects are strictly limited to the lonely poet: "My lonely Anguish melts no Heart, but mine." Here as in the "Ode on the Spring" and the Eton College ode we discover the lonely poet who has nothing to offer mankind. The teeming world of the fields producing "their wonted Tribute," the birds warming "their little Loves," and the cheerful existence of happier men contrast markedly with the barrenness of the speaker's present mood. His sorrow, akin to pure negation, can only take shape by comparing it with the joy around him. The "other Notes" and "different Object" repined for and required remain obscure, but suggest strains of mourning and weeping and the dead Richard West. Gray goes even further. His mourning, in contrast to the "smileing Mornings," is fruitless, and so he weeps the more because of the emptiness and worthlessness of that grief.

Here Gray tacitly questions the value of the personal voice, of
the sincerely expressed grief. The world as poets have known it,
warmed by "redning Phoebus" and dressed in "green Attire" is the
world which brings pleasure to men. "Lonely Anguish," however, is
subjective, empty, even though it might be true and, finally,
inexpressible. The imitative mode has, on the other hand, a full
vocabulary suited to communication, tried and tested in the world.

Once again, as in his odes, Gray engages himself in dialogue,
searching for an appropriate diction and questioning its validity
once it is found. Just as the speaker in the odes came to question
the value of all that he had expounded earlier, here the speaker
questions the value of the sentiments expressed, the language used
and, ultimately, of the experience of sincere grief itself.

Here, as usual, Gray associates melancholy or grief with "real"
experience, since it characterizes his every thought and action.
But, then, he questions the validity of his own understanding of
things and of the value of that understanding and consequent expression. It is at this point, however, where his own experience
diverges from that of most men, that he seems to waver between
confidence in himself and confidence in tradition. To put the
question in the form most appropriate to the purpose of this paper:
he cannot decide whether to be an imitator or an original.

The importance Gray gave to this problem can be seen best in The
Bard. Just before the bard hurls himself from Mt. Snowdon, he
compares his own state with that of King Edward:

>'Enough for me: With joy I see
>'The different doom our Fates assign.
>'Be thine Despair, and scept'red Care,
>'To triumph, and to die, are mine."(139-42)

But is this "triumph" convincing? I think not. Most obviously the
triumph is linked with self-destruction, a fact the final couplet
makes extraordinarily vivid: "He spoke, and headlong from the
mountain's height / Deep in the roaring tide he plung'd to endless
night." (143-44) "Endless night" suggests at best the very antithesis of what is usually associated with triumph.[34] Indeed, even
during the lengthy cursing of Edward and his line, the reader is
painfully aware that the bard is experiencing much of the suffering
which he calls down on the hapless king. All of Edward's family
and friends are to be taken from him and he is to die alone:

> "Low on his funeral couch he lies!
> "No pitying heart, no eye, afford
> "A tear to grace his obsequies. (64-66)

Now the bard, I suspect, like Gray, has no family, and, placing his entire reliance on his fellow poets, who have been slain, he too dies alone:

> 'Dear lost companions of my tuneful art,
> 'Dear, as the light that visits these sad eyes,
> 'Dear, as the ruddy drops that warm my heart,
> 'Ye died amidst your dying country's cries --
>                           (38-42)

Their ghosts, of course, appear and join the bard in cursing Edward, but when that is done, disappear, leaving him alone:

> 'Stay, oh stay! nor thus forlorn
> 'Leave me unbless'd, unpitied, here to mourn . . .
>                           (101-102)

Here again is the theme of lonely anguish so important in the sonnet to West.

The triumph of the bard, such as it is, comes not merely in the predicted downfall of Edward and the rise of the House of Tudor, but more specifically in the greatness to be achieved by future poets. But the vision of the future is short and, after Shakespeare and Milton, indeterminate. "Distant," "lessen," "lost," and "expire" set the tone of the dismal conclusion:

> 'And distant warblings lessen on my ear,
> 'That lost in long futurity expire. (133-34)

This accords with Gray's rather pessimistic view of poetry in his own age and particularly of the decline of the English language, which, he wrote in 1742, is "too diffuse, & daily grows more & more enervate."[35]

The point I wish to emphasize here is the extreme ambiguity surrounding the bard's death. Momentary satisfaction can be gained from the prospect of some future greatness for poetry, or for Gray and the reader, the affirmation of Shakespeare and Milton; but the bard's plunge to "endless night" leaves us to wonder whether the hopes for the future are not merely a deception, if moments of greatness are not glimmering preludes to the ineluctable descent. As in the poems discussed earlier, the moral values presented are called in question. The fate of the bard and the uncertainty of his visions suggest a triumph which can only be gained in death. From Gray's viewpoint, I believe, that is a very questionable triumph indeed.[36] Death, then, no matter how sublime it may be in this poem, is the melancholy end which calls in question every serious act of intellect and imagination. It is death, without the grandeur of sublimity, which is the subject of An Elegy Written in a Country Church-yard.

> The Curfew tolls the knell of parting day,
> The lowing herd wind slowly o'er the lea,
> The plowman homeward plods his weary way,
> And leaves the world to darkness and to me. (1-4)

Here in the opening stanza we have the first and last direct reference by the speaker to himself. Since he is left in the dark, perhaps it is appropriate that the search for himself which follows be conducted in impersonal dialogue. The generalized impersonality begins directly in the next line: "Now fades the glimmering landscape on the sight . . ." It would have been easy for Gray to write: "Now fades the glimmering landscape on my sight," but apparently the movement away from self was important enough to make clear very early in the poem.

As the speaker proceeds to set up his moral polarities, with the dead of power and fortune on the one side and the humble and good on the other, the poet's curiously intermediate position is defined. The humble dead are remembered neither for their power nor their poetry; since all opportunity was denied them:

> Perhaps in this neglected spot is laid
> Some heart once pregnant with celestial fire;
> Hands, that the rod of empire might have sway'd,
> Or wak'd to extasy the living lyre. (45-48)

The possible guilt of poets, though falling short of that assumed by men of power, is made clear. The humble dead's lot forbad

> The struggling pangs of conscious truth to hide,
> To quench the blushes of ingenuous shame,
> Or heap the shrine of Luxury and Pride
> With incense kindled at the Muse's flame. (69-72)

In short, the poet, in seeking after honor and immortality, may be a collaborator with the forces of tyranny; thus we see why, even at his best, the poet is: "Beneath the Good how far -- ."[37]

The poet, then, by placing importance in fame and the art of poetry is neglecting the true values of humanity. This is the point of the stanzas on the rustic poetry on the gravestones:

> Yet ev'n these bones from insult to protect
> Some frail memorial still erected nigh,
> With uncouth rhimes and shapeless sculpture deck'd,
> Implores the passing tribute of a sigh.
>
> Their name, their years, spelt by th'unletter'd muse,
> The place of fame and elegy supply:
> And many a holy text around she strews,
> That teach the rustic moralist to die. (77-84)

Here is truly sincere poetry, careless in spelling, carelessly strewing about holy texts; but serving one of the highest human functions, i.e., teaching men how to die. Somehow all the elaborate morality of Gray's poems pales before this simplicity, and Gray seems conscious of it.

The poet in the poem, no matter how honest his attempt to understand his relationship to poetry and mankind, is never at one with his humble subject, as is made clear when the inward colloquy takes clear shape:

> For thee, who mindful of th'unhonour'd Dead
> Dost in these lines their artless tale relate; . . .
> (93-94)

Though the speaker is mindful of the humble dead, the emphasis on the artlessness of _their_ tale implies the artfulness of his relation of it. Further, the answer by the hoary-headed Swain to the kindred Spirit's question reveals the spiritual distance between poet and rustic. The swain recalls that

> 'Mutt'ring his wayward fancies he would rove,
> 'Now drooping, woeful wan, like one forlorn,
> 'Or craz'd with care, or cross'd in hopeless love.
> (106-8)

The swain's search for a reason for the poet's behavior, i.e., he is forlorn or crazed with care, or last (and perhaps best), a star-crossed lover, betrays an expected incapacity to understand sympathetically the characteristic melancholy of the serious poet.

If the poet is (whether he likes it or not) beyond the comprehension of the good people he seems to value most, and if he is the artful poet yearning for artless simplicity, then the epitaph is curiously inappropriate:

> Here rests his head upon the lap of Earth
> A Youth to Fortune and to Fame unknown,
> Fair Science frown'd not on his humble birth,
> And Melancholy mark'd him for her own. (117-20)

Neither Richard West, nor Gray, nor, apparently, the poet-speaker was a youth unknown to <u>both</u> fame and fortune.[38] West's birth was certainly not humble; and Gray would not have regarded his own as such. Only melancholy is a common denominator:

> Large was his bounty, and his soul sincere,
> Heav'd did a recompence as largely send:
> He gave to Mis'ry all he had, a tear,
> He gain'd from Heav'n ('twas all he wish'd) a friend.
> (121-24)

Here again the epitaph seems not to agree with our understanding of the poet-speaker as distinct from the humble, guileless people whose memorial he has erected in the poem. The chief tension is precisely that the poet is not sincere and bountiful -- at one with Heaven. The epitaph, then, is an expressed hope rather than a realized fact. The poet does in the epitaph attain a oneness with those whose lives are most highly valued. "The paths of glory" (even poetic glory, such as it is) "lead but to the grave," the common end. In the epitaph, then, in death, the outsider poet is integrated into the true community of men, remembered not so much for what he was, but what he wished to be. Like the Bard, his triumph comes only in "endless night."

Thus the dialogue between the learned poet of imitation and the sincere voice of the self is concluded, giving the verdict to the latter, but demonstrating, in the failure to achieve the single voice of the poet's sole self and the realization of some of that potential only in death, the impossibility of the task assigned. Gray's commitment to imitation and learning is too great to allow a simpler social consciousness. The way for that can be cleared only by his death.

What I propose here is that Gray's best poems present an inward colloquy between the personated or imitative voices of Gray and that single, serious voice which Plato thought everyone should have, the voice we use to speak to God and the person we love. This is the voice of our religious and social being. This voice, however, is skeptical and regardless of tradition. It inquires after a social reality quite different from that sanctioned by the imitative mode, a reality characterized by simplicity and sincerity.

For extremely complex reasons, barely touched upon here, English poets at mid-century were struggling toward that voice and that reality. The attempts are often grotesque, as if the poets cannot make up their minds which way to go. To throw off the influence of the classical tradition is to leave oneself with an unsatisfactory trust in nature and simple sentiment. On the other hand, to imitate is to lose one's voice, or to make certain that it could never be found. Gray, unlike many of his contemporaries, is able to capitalize on this tension, to make poetry out of it. Later, in turning away from this struggle toward more strictly imitative modes, his poetry begins to fail him. But in his earlier and sometimes great poetry, the subject of this essay, there is a kind of schizophrenia which results in two intentions -- the one at odds with the other. Perhaps it was this confusion between imitation and originality which made poetic composition at mid-century such a precarious occupation.

Yale University

## NOTES

1. *The Republic of Plato*, trans. Allan Bloom (New York, 1968), p. 71. This new literal translation is likely to become the authoritative English text. Citations to the Greek text are to The Loeb Classical Library edition, p. 224.

2. Thomas Gray, *The Works*, ed. Edmund Gosse (London, 1884), IV, 233.

3. "Poetry as an Imitative Art" in *Aristotle's Poetics and English Literature*, ed. Elder Olson (Chicago, 1965), p. 57.

4. Gray asked Wharton's view of the latter work. See *Correspondence*, ed. Paget Toynbee and Leonard Whibley (Oxford, 1935), pp. 531-32.

5. *Works* (London, 1811), II, 129.

6. *Ibid.*, II, 129-130.

7. *Ibid.*, II, 176-177.

8. *Ibid.*, II, 145.

9. *Ibid.*, II, 213.

10. *Ibid.*, II, 232.

11. *Conjectures on Original Composition* in *Criticism: Twenty Major Statements*, ed. Charles Kaplan (San Francisco, n.d.), p. 215.

12. *Observations on the Writings and on the Character of Mr. Gray* (London, 1815), p. 75.

13. *Correspondence*, pp. 532-533. *Pastor Cum traheret* is, of course, the XVth Ode of Horace's First Book. The ode takes the form of Nereus's prophecy, "...caneret fera Nereus fata," and may in turn be an imitation of Proteus's account to Menelaus, *Odyssey*, IV, 472-537. See J.L. Lincoln, *Works of Horace* (New York, 1866), p. 330.

14. *Ibid.*, p. 571.

15. *Ibid.*, p. 541.

16. *Ibid.*, p. 1169.

17. *Ibid.*, p. 566.

18. *The Republic*, p. 75. Loeb Library, p. 240.

19. *Ibid.*, p. 76. Loeb Library, p. 242.

20. *Ibid.*, p. 75. Loeb Library, p. 240.

21. *The Formal Strain: Studies in Augustan Imitation and Satire* (Chicago, 1969), pp. 113-128.

22. I am fully aware that for some readers these speculations will require a good deal of evidence. Needless to say, elaborate studies of all these poets are not feasible here. I commit myself on this difficult issue only to suggest further possible meanings for this study of Gray. An essay suggestive of some of these directions is W.J. Bate, "The English Poet and the Burden of the Past, 1660-1820" in *Aspects of the Eighteenth Century*, ed. Earl Wasserman (Baltimore, 1965), pp. 245-264.

23. "Imitation as Freedom -- 1717-1798," read at the English Institute, September 1968. Mr. Wimsatt has been kind enough to allow me the use of this valuable essay which, I trust, will soon be published.

24. *Essays and Criticisms by Thomas Gray*, ed. C.S. Northrup (Boston and London, 1911), pp. 120-121. Another use by Gray of Plato's distinction between narration and imitation can be found in a letter to Walpole, January 2, 1761, in which he comments on *Julie ou la Nouvelle Héloïse*: "Rousseau's people do not interest me; there is but one character and one style in them all, I do not know their faces asunder." *Horace Walpole's Correspondence*, ed. W.S. Lewis, XIV (New Haven, 1948), p. 118.

25. *Essays in Criticism*, XIII (1963), 222.

26. *Ibid.*, p. 227.

27. "On a Special Decorum in Gray's Elegy" in *From Sensibility to Romanticism*, eds. F.W. Hilles and Harold Bloom (New York, 1965), p. 172.

28. *Ibid.*, p. 172.

29. *Ibid.*, p. 172.

30. All citations to Gray's poems are to *The Complete Poems of Thomas Gray*, ed. H.W. Starr and J.R. Hendrickson (Oxford, 1966). Line numbers are included in the text.

31. Such echoes suggest imitation of other poets, a kind of imitation different from that expounded in the *Republic*, and derived from neo-classical authors, particularly Quintilian.

32. *Complete Poems*, p. 207.

33. *Augustan Studies* (London, 1961), p. 88.

34. It is the same Teiresias-like punishment inflicted on Milton and described in "The Progress of Poesy":

>     He saw; but blasted with excess of light,
>     Closed his eyes in endless night. (101-02)

35. *Correspondence*, p. 196.

36. If Norton Nicholl's report that Gray said "Why I felt myself the bard" is accurate in all its implications, my point would seem to be further substantiated. Gray's melancholy was far from being merely a literary device, and may be found implicit in some of his most triumphant and self-righteous assertions. See *Correspondence*, p. 1290.

37. "Progress of Poesy," l. 123.

38. The only necessary assumption here is that the subject of the epitaph, on whose humble birth "Fair Science frown'd not," is *not* the so-called stonecutter poet inspired by "th'unletter'd muse . . . ." John H. Sutherland is particularly persuasive on this point. See his "The Stonecutter in Gray's'Elegy'," *Modern Philology*, LV (1957-58), 11-13.

AUGUSTAN IMITATION: THE ROLE OF THE ORIGINAL

By Howard D. Weinbrot

Augustan Imitation takes several forms.[1] An imitator, for example, may modernize the allusions, names, and places in the parent-poem while largely being faithful to its sense and meaning. Thus John Oldham describes his Imitation of the *Ars poetica* (1681), alludes to other translators' works, insists that though he has taken a few minor liberties he has been "religiously strict to its sense," and makes clear that by Imitation he means a paraphrased and modernized poem. The Imitation, he says, was forced upon him, for though Ben Jonson and Roscommon had excellently translated the work, they had not exhausted the possibilities of translation. He imagined that he could improve the poem for the modern reader "by putting <u>Horace</u> into a more modern Dress than hitherto he has appeared in; that is, by making him speak as if he were living and writing now. I therefore resolved to alter the Scene from <u>Rome</u> to <u>London</u>, and to make use of <u>English</u> Names of Men, Places, and Customs, where the Parallel would decently permit, which I conceived would give a kind of new Air to the Poem and render it more agreeable to the relish of the present Age."[2] Any omissions, Oldham says, are likely to be from "Passages not much material" and would not offend the original author. This form of Imitation, then, is similar to paraphrastic translation; the modern poet subjects his creative interests to those of the original author.

Another kind of Imitation modernizes or silently drops archaic references where necessary, is largely faithful to the original but, nevertheless, drastically alters it by means of truncation as, specifically, in Cowley's version of Horace's "Epodon" (Epode II) (1668). In Horace's poem Alfius, an usurer, relates the glories of the country life to which he intends to retire and, along the way, celebrates the fertility of the fields, the beauty of the country, the pleasures of hunting, and the virtues of a humble, chaste wife who prepares wholesome native dishes. When this speech is over, Horace comments not only upon Alfius, but also upon the nature of man's wishes and accomplishments: "When the usurer Alfius had uttered this, on the very point of beginning the farmer's life, he called in all his funds upon the Ides -- and on the Kalends seeks to put them out again." Cowley's version is fairly close to Horace's; but he excludes the speaker's profession and the final ironic stanza, thereby changes the tone and "moral" of his original, and makes his Imitation bluntly didactic and a consistently developed discourse on its opening couplet: "Happy the Man whom bounteous Gods allow With his own Hands Paternal Grounds to Plough!"[3]

In a third kind of Imitation the poet freely imitates all (or most) of the parent-poem, and yet decreases his own and his readers' dependence upon the source. Rochester's *Timon* (1674), for instance, is a free Imitation of Boileau's Third Satire which, in turn, is a free Imitation of Horace *Satires* ii. 8. *Timon* clearly has French and Roman precedent; but it does not make extensive use of that precedent as an element of its own structure. Rochester's *Satyr Against Mankind* (1675) is an even freer adaptation of Boileau's Eighth Satire. Rochester preserves some of Boileau's ideas -- the attack on man's reason and the superiority of animals, for instance -- and thereby keeps the reader aware of Boileau's poem.[4] Johnson thus observes both the presence of the original and Rochester's alterations when, somewhat disparagingly, he says: "Of the Satyr against Man Rochester can only claim what remains when all Boileau's part is taken away."[5] But, as John F. Moore has shown, Rochester's poem lacks "any sustained verbal parallel" with Boileau's and "not one idea" of the Eighth Satire "has been used by Rochester without important alterations."[6] In short, it would be difficult, if not impossible, to print the parallel passages of the parent-poem as Pope or Johnson did or in fact, as was done in 1714 with Rochester's own "Allusion to Horace" (1676), a closer section-by-section (but really not close) Imitation of Horace, *Satires* i.10. Indeed, so independent is the *Satyr* that in October of 1682 Oldham, an admirer of Rochester, wrote "The Eighth Satyr of Monsieur Boileau, Imitated." Apparently Rochester's poem was so different from Boileau's that Oldham did not believe that his new attempt competed with Rochester's or needed justification.

We have, then, three different modes of the Imitation: (1) paraphrase and consistent modernization of an announced model (as in Oldham's *Ars Poetica*); (2) overt citation of the original, together with free translation of *part* of the poem which, thereby, alters the poem's meaning (as in Cowley's "Epodon"); (3) extremely free Imitation of an unannounced source which, nevertheless, the poet expected the reader to know (Rochester's *Satyr against Mankind*). None of these, however, is wholly representative of the greatest examples of Augustan Imitation: those of Pope and Johnson, in which the original is incorporated into the modern-poet's poem. The original may serve as a source of comparison, contrast, or both; or it may be a norm against which the modern may be judged; it may be judged against the modern norm; or, at different moments, be both. Similarly, the original poem may serve to support the concept of general nature and show the timelessness of important human concerns; or it may portray a modern advance in areas of ethics and conduct untouched by the earlier author. The Augustan Imitation at its best is aware of the many aspects and voices of history, of the power of example,

and the value of an expansive, non-insular, poetic imagination. Much
of this power has been characterized obliquely in Samuel Johnson's
comments on Dryden's Essay on Dramatick Poesy (1668): "Dryden at
least imported his science, and gave his country what it wanted
before," he says, and then adds an essential correction: "or rather,
he imported only the materials, and manufactured them by his own
skill."[7] Pope and Johnson as Imitators want the reader to be equally
aware of the imported goods and the skill of their domestic manufacture,
and as a result insist upon a dimension of response not possible for
the three imitative modes described above. Pope and Johnson generally
chose to adapt complete Roman poems and altered or followed and exalted
or demeaned the parent-poem as their own purposes demanded. The imitator as modernizer largely serves his author's intention not his own;
the extremely free imitator is likely to lose the pleasure of comparison;
and even the partial imitator often is a paraphrastic translator during
the part of the poem imitated, and does not care whether the reader is
aware of the portion of the poem he excludes. That is missing in each
of these forms is at the heart of the genius and originality of Pope's
and Johnson's Imitations: the presence of the original and the way
in which an earlier culture, metaphor, or device of structure becomes
raw material for the modern poet's use. Of course numerous critics
from Pope's age to our own have been aware of the Imitator's source.
Too often, however, critics of, say, Pope's Imitations have chosen to
measure Pope against Horace instead, especially after 1734,[8] of Horace
against Pope. They have thus both limited the metaphorical range
and power of the imitator and his Imitation. It would, to take an
extreme case, hardly do to compare and contrast Boileau's Ode sur la
prise de Namur (1692) with Prior's English Ballad, on the Taking of
Namur (1695) and conclude that Boileau is a better poet than Prior.
Proper analysis of this parody-Imitation should suggest that Boileau
is a poet in willing bondage to his King and Court, has betrayed truth,
made a mockery of genuine epic conventions, and is merely inflated
when he pretends to be elevated. It is, in part, because Boileau is
a good poet that the Ode is a bad poem; that is, Prior's Ballad makes
clear, a noble satirist has surrendered his integrity to the corrupt
Court. Prior's Imitation thus deflates the cultural and military
pretensions of an entire culture and its spokesman, and the high
quality of Boileau's untruthful panegyric verse is set against the
rough but truthful English Imitation. Hence Boileau says:

> Dans ses chansons immortelles,
> Comme un Aigle audacieux,
> PINDARE étendant ses aisles,
> Fuit loin des Vulgaires yeux.
> Mais, ô ma fidele Lyre,
> Si, dans l'ardeur qui m'inspire,
> Tu peux suivre mes Transports;
> Les chesnes des Monts de Thrace
> N'ont rien oüi, que n'efface
> La douceur de tes accords (ll. 11-20).

Prior takes the central concepts of Pindaric poetic flights and the
faithful lyre inspired by nobility, and gives them rather a different
turn:

> PINDAR, that Eagle, mounts the Skies;
>     While Virtue leads the noble Way:
> Too like a Vultur BOILEAU flies,
>     Where sordid Interest shows the Prey.
> When once the Poet's Honour ceases,
>     From Reason far his Transports rove:
> And BOILEAU, for eight hundred Pieces,
>     Makes LOUIS take the Wall of JOVE (ll. 13-20).[9]

In order to understand the Imitation, then we must understand its
relationship with the parent-poem. In the case of Prior and Boileau
it is one of hostility and rejection; in the case of Johnson's
London (1738) it is one of symbiosis. Johnson imitates Juvenal's
Third Satire, in which the satirist Juvenal accompanies his depart-
ing friend Umbricius to the gates of Rome. In Johnson's Imitation
Thales is about to cross the Thames and leave London. As a modern
Englishman, Thales is no longer talking to a famous Roman satirist
but an anonymous English friend who will soon learn the painful
lesson that, spiritually or literally, London destroys those who
stay within its cursed walls. Indeed, the need to modernize and
shift from Rome to London provides a subdued but essential metaphor
in the poem, since London now appears to be so heinous that only comparison with Domitian's Rome can do it full justice. It also implies
the parallel of decay and fall as a result of corruption and makes
clear that Thales, like his forebear, is not a mere alarmist who
leaves when he should attempt to reform the city. Presumably, Thales
knows from Juvenal that destruction of Roman values induced the
destruction of Rome; and he also knows that there was hope for the
true Roman who sought, found, and propagated the older values still
to be found in the country-retreat. Hence in the conclusion to London
he portrays the vigorous continuation of satire against the nation
and its rulers when Thales and his friend reunite sometime in the
reasonably near future. Much of the little hope there is for a
revived world in London stems from the precedent in Juvenal's poem
when, after the desired comparison with the original, we judge that
what could be done then can be done, or at least attempted to be done,
now. The city and its corrupt citizens may be destroying themselves;
but their initial greatness may be preserved within the individual's
mind, heart, and actions in a rural setting. Without the Juvenalian
resonance London loses much of its metaphorical and historical power.

One should understand more than the relationship between the original
and the Imitation and the setting or plot of the parent-poem; one
should also know the text that the modern poet used, since even a
single word may affect the imitator's tone and strategy. At the end
of London, for example, Thales says to his friend:

> Farewell!--When youth, and health, and fortune spent,
> Thou fly'st for refuge to the wilds of Kent;
> And tired like me with follies and with crimes,
> In angry numbers warn'st succeeding times;
> Then shall thy friend, nor thou refuse his aid,
> Still foe to vice, forsake his Cambrian shade;
> In virtue's cause once more exert his rage,
> Thy satire point, and animate thy page (ll. 256-263).[10]

The character of the speaker of this passage seems to me objectionable. He implies that the friend will leave London only after he is thoroughly defeated, whereas the more clever Thales leaves with some of his fortune and much of his vigor. Moreover, the friend appears to be an inferior poet who needs Thales' insistent pointing and animating before his satire is poetically acceptable. However offensive the section may be, the last couplet, at least, depends upon an important textual crux. _Satirarum ego, ni pudet illas, / Adjutor gelidos veniam caligatus in agros_, are the lines reproduced at the foot of Johnson's page. The text Johnson used, the translations of Stapylton, Holyday, and Dryden, and the Latin edition of Rigaltius all use the word _adjutor_ in the final line of Juvenal's Third Satire.[11] Though _auditor_ was then a variant for _adjutor_, it was not fully accepted until the late nineteenth and early twentieth centuries. The Loeb text thus portrays Umbricius visiting his friend and _listening_ to his satires "if they think me worthy of that honor,"[12] whereas Johnson puts Thales (who, after all, is addressing an unnamed speaker rather than the satirist Juvenal) into the role of helper. In his prose gloss of this line Prateus uses the phrase "Satyrarum auxiliator," and only in his notes to the passage observes that "Nonnulli codices habent, _auditor_."[13]

Awareness of the original's rhetorical situation and its text, then, can influence the Imitator's poem and our understanding of it. In some cases the changes made merely indicate adaptation of names and places; but in others they suggest essential clues to understanding. The latter is the case in Pope's _Epistle to Augustus_ (1737) and Johnson's _Vanity of Human Wishes_ (1749).

To read an "original" Imitation properly, we have seen, one should be aware not only of the poet's adherence to the parent-poem, but his divergence from it as well. Indeed, in certain circumstances he might diverge by adhering. Specifically, the opening paragraph of Pope's _Epistle to Augustus_ is a close adaptation of Horace's praise of Augustus Caesar's military strength abroad, and stable moral, government at home; the same lines when applied to George Augustus, King of England are wildly inappropriate, include sexual puns ("Your Country, chief, in Arms abroad defend" [l. 3]),[14] and announce the theme of inversion not only of the dignity and military strength of the true Augustan world, but of the roles of the King or Emperor and the poet. Moreover, it is not only the English court but, at times, Horace and Rome who are satirized.

The errors of the public in Horace's epistle are aesthetic in nature. Horace separates political from poetic concerns, so that the foolish artistic judgments contrast (from his point of view) with the intelligent political ones. In fact much of the intention of the poem is to urge Augustus to lead the public to honor today's good poets as they honor today's good Emperor. The public so loyal to Caesar is strangely fickle in its literary tastes; this is particularly unfortunate, since Caesar himself is a good judge of poetry and chooses Virgil and Varius, the finest modern poets, to sing his deserved rewards.

For Pope, however, bad political judgments are a function of bad poetic judgments (and vice-versa); the people who revere bad old and new poets also revere the bad king. "Some monster of a king" (l. 210) sits on the British throne and receives praise, while "The many-headed Monster of the pit" (l. 305) debases the drama by calling for farce and pageantry. Horace believes that the Romans, "so wise and just" in praising Caesar "judge all other things by a wholly different rule and method."[15] Pope believes that the English are equally foolish in both judgments, and he shows not only that the Lords are corrupt ("Farce [was] once the taste of Mobs, but now of Lords" [l. 311] ) and help to corrupt the people, but that the fountain of corruption is the King himself. It is not only that the stage pageants portray and debase "Peers, Heralds, Bishops, Ermine, Gold, and Lawn" (l. 317); nor only that "Old Edward's Armour beams on Cibber's breast" (l. 319), thus making clear that even England's mythic princes have been degraded during the present reign;[16] but primarily because Pope's remark regarding Charles II is equally true of George II -- ad exemplum regis:[17]

>   In every Taste of foreign Courts improv'd,
>   All, by the King's Example, liv'd and lov'd (ll. 141-142).

Horace hopes that Caesar will encourage more good modern non-dramatic authors, and that the Roman people will emulate Augustus. Pope fears that in his age such emulation has already taken place, and that King, Court, and Country have been ruined as a result. Horace ends his poem by associating himself with Augustus, since neither would want to be praised by poor poets, have such burdensome and misshapen stuff remembered about him, and have the indignity of seeing the verse and, symbolically, himself used to wrap grocer's wares. Pope, however, dissociates himself from George, insists that "A vile Encomium doubly ridicules" (l. 41), and that "Praise undeserv'd is scandal in disguise" (l. 413). He finally says:

> When I flatter, let my dirty leaves
> (Like Journals, Odes, and such forgotten things
> As Eusden, Philips, Settle, writ of Kings)
> Cloath spice, line trunks, or flutt'ring in a row,
> Befringe the rails of Bedlam and Sohoe (ll. 415-419).

Horace does not want his Emperor subjected to the indignity that Pope describes his as already having suffered. George has inspired the bad poems of bad poets and, accordingly, has been doubly ridiculed, scandalized, and symbolically disgraced through a less than royal use of the sheets of printed poetry.

Pope, then, portrays the literary taste of the British King and people as unfortunately different from that of Augustus, if not Augustan citizens. But he also portrays "Pope" as different from "Horace" and, as one might expect from the rejection of Horace in the first <u>Dialogue</u> of the <u>Epilogue to the Satires</u> (1738) written shortly thereafter, as superior in an important way. Pope was always aware that, unlike Boileau and Horace, he was "Unplaced, unpensioned, no man's heir, or slave;" he was not the defender of the crown but, under present circumstances, its attacker. Horace serves as an aesthetic norm but, particularly after about 1734, is often suspect as a political, ethical, or religious norm. Hence, though Pope thought "An Answer from Horace" of greater authority in <u>The First Satire of the Second Book, Imitated</u> (1733), he thinks rather less of Horace in the <u>Epistle to Augustus</u>. In his Advertisement, for example, he remarks:

> [Horace] paints [his Prince] with all the great and good Qualities of a Monarch, upon whom the <u>Romans</u> depended for the Encrease of an <u>Absolute Empire</u>. But to make the Poem entirely English, I was willing to add one or two of those Virtues which contribute to the Happiness of a <u>Free People</u>, and are more consistent with the Welfare of our Neighbours (p. 191; italics and roman type reversed).

We thus realize that George Augustus is likened to a Roman absolute monarch, while the virtues "added" belong to the English people (though Pope is probably also attacking George II for sacrificing English to Hanoverian interests). The people are concerned with "the Welfare of our Neighbours," while the Monarch is concerned with "the Encrease of an <u>Absolute Empire</u>." The people and their King are thus set apart. Pope clearly sees the nature of his King, whereas Horace's perceptions and honesty are compromised. The word <u>paint</u>, for example, is surely ambiguous. It includes, Johnson says in the <u>Dictionary</u>, this meaning: "To deck with artificial colours." In Pope's view, Horace is unjustifiably praising a tyrant who, it was commonly thought, under the guise of stability and order, was one of the destroyers of Republican atandards and freedom.[18] Pope's friend Lyttleton, for example, describes the Augustan age as an era of "the final settlement of the <u>Imperial</u> power, another species of despotism, no less violently assumed, but more moderately exercised, and more artfully constituted, by Augustus Caesar."[19] And in his <u>Dialogues of the Dead</u> (1760), Lyttleton's Cato characterizes Augustus as a tyrant, violator of law, trust, friendship, and the values which made the Republic great. Even Messalla, the adversarius, agrees that "Octavius had done all you said," and merely argues that he was the best dictator to have under the circumstances.[20] Perhaps of even greater importance, however, is their exchange regarding the state of the arts under Augustus. "Under Augustus' judicious patronage, the Muses made Rome their capital seat. It would have pleased you to have known Virgil, Horace, Tibullus, Ovid, Livy, and many more, whose names will be illustrious to all generations," Mesalla argues. But Cato insists that he would not be pleased, and in the process denigrates letters if they come at the cost of liberty. "Your Augustus and you," Cato insists, "after the ruin of our liberty, made Rome a Greek city, an academy of fine wits, another Athens under the government of Demetrius Phalareus. I would much rather have seen her under Fabricius and Curius, and her other honest old consuls, who could not read."[21]

Horace thus emerges as a poet who flatters an absolute prince; he helps to add counterfeit or painted luster to the pernicious government. Pope, in contrast (ll. 189-240), is the revolutionary who seeks not merely a change of kings, but a change in ethical values. Under the mask of the obedient poet, Pope attacks the court, flatterers, and their illicit bases of power, and praises Swift because "The Rights a Court attack'd a Poet sav'd" (l. 224). In the parent-poem, then, Augustus is a good patron of the arts whom Horace, a great poet, hopes to make better so that he will, in turn, improve the taste of his people. As Pope sees it, Augustus himself is a tyrant and Horace his servant; both are as tainted ethically and politically as they are exalted in art and literary judgment. Thus in the Imitation Pope subtly contrasts his own independence with Horace's bondage, and George II's barbaric taste with Augustus' elegance. Pope's Advertisement characterizes Horace as urging Augustus to understand that "Poets, under due Regulations, were in many respects useful to the <u>State</u>" (p. 254); that is, useful to Augustus' despotic government. And he also suggests, obliquely to be sure, that Augustus' tyranny leads to the decay of Roman arts and letters, since it imprisons art in the government's standards; this decay, in fact, is already being recreated in the new

Augustan age. The Epistle to Augustus is perhaps the most complex of Augustan Imitations. At various points it will attack Horace, Augustus, King George, or the English people; and at various other points it will use Horace and Augustus as norms. It is, finally, fully comprehensible only when we have reclaimed Pope's conception of Horace's poem.

Pope's Imitation thus adheres to Horace's poem and diverges from it, as Pope imports material that is generally known and weaves it on his own looms. Samuel Johnson employs a similar method in The Vanity of Human Wishes, where independence and awareness of one's source are also important. The misunderstood Democritus passage (ll. 49-72) in that poem makes his procedure clear. One critic, mistaking divergence for adherence, observes:

> Juvenal invokes the laughing and the weeping sages, Democritus and Heraclitus; but it is the pitiless laughter of Democritus that rings through the poem. Juvenal's mood is one of derision, of 'cutting irony.' Johnson unsuitably retains the long passage addressed to Democritus . . . . Here for once the palimpsest is transparent. At no time did Johnson conceive of life as an 'eternal jest.' The echo from Juvenal is quite at variance with his own voice in the rest of the poem.[22]

Of course Johnson did not regard life as an eternal jest; nor does he say so in the poem. It is Democritus who says that and who echoes Juvenal, whereas "Johnson," or the speaker, clearly rejects the Juvenalian and the Democritan view.[23]

Juvenal introduces Democritus after attacking the wish for gold. Once the reader realizes the terrible consequences of such a fulfilled wish, Juvenal asks, "will you not commend the two wise men, one of whom [Democritus] would laugh while the opposite sage [Heraclitus] would weep every time he set a foot outside the door?" (ll. 28-30) Juvenal answers the question at once: "To condemn by a cutting laugh comes readily to us all; the wonder is how the other sage's eyes were supplied with all that water" (ll. 31-32). And shortly thereafter he adds that Democritus "laughed at the troubles, ay and at the pleasures, of the crowd, sometimes too at their tears" (ll. 51-52). Juvenal decides that Democritus' wisdom "shows us that men of high distinction and destined to be great examples may be born in a dullard air, and in [Abdera, in Thrace] the land of mutton heads" (ll. 48-50). From here to the conclusion of the poem it is the unceasingly harsh, savage, mockery of Democritus which characterizes Juvenal's tone and extends even to the value of human prayer which he regards as frankly irrelevant -- "What I commend to you [to pray for], you can give to yourself" -- and to the divinity of the gods: "Thou wouldst have no divinity, O Fortune, if we had but wisdom; it is we that make a goddess of thee, and place thee in the skies" (ll. 365-366).[24]

Johnson invites us to see a Democritus who is different from Juvenal's: he is earthbound and therefore limited in vision, improperly cynical, malicious, superficial, and hardly a man of high distinction and great example. We hear, for instance, that Johnson's Democritus will "arise on earth" (l. 49), that he regards men as fools and life as an "eternal jest" (l. 52), that he laughs at man enchained by poverty, crushed by toil, and dying in lonely isolation (ll. 53-55). Though he tries to discern "truth and nature," the pagan, cynic, assumptions he holds make this impossible. He has a "philosophic eye" (l. 64) rather than a Christian one, and so regards the world as a "farce" able to maintain his "mirth" (l. 67). To repeat, this is Democritus' viewpoint, not Johnson's. Johnson eliminates Juvenal's praise of the pagan philosopher, asks us to evaluate it and, while asking, implies that we will find it inadequate:

> Such was the scorn that fill'd the sage's mind,
> Renew'd at ev'ry glance on human kind;
> How just that scorn ere yet thy voice declare,
> Search every state, and canvass ev'ry prayer (ll. 69-72).

Democritus' view was based merely upon glances -- "to view with a quick cast of the eye" (Dictionary) -- whereas we are to search and canvass both external and internal, the affairs of men and their secret wishes. We are thus called upon to evaluate the accuracy of Democritus' concept of life as a farce. That form of drama, Johnson says in the Dictionary is: "A dramatick representation written without regularity, and stuffed with wild and ludicrous conceits." And he cites this illustrative quotation from Dryden's Preface to Dufresnoy (1695): "a farce is that in poetry which grotesque is in a picture: the persons and actions of a farce are all unnatural, and the manners false; that is, inconsistent with the characters of mankind."[25] Democritus' pagan, superficial view misrepresents the true nature of man and cannot even comprehend the nature of God. Hence he inffectually attempts to "pierce each scene with philosophic eye," while the man who rejects the cynical view will be "Safe in his pow'r whose eyes discern afar" (l. 354). Moreover, the "scorn" that fills "the sage's mind" has unchristian associations for Johnson. It is the trait of the evil man in Job xvi.20, which Johnson cites under To scorn: "My friends scorn me; but mine eyes poureth out tears unto God." And this is what the Christian fears in Psalms xxviii, 1, since, whether the scorn be his own or God's, it cuts him off from grace and a possible audience with God. Johnson cites this under the noun scorn: "Unto thee will I cry, O Lord! think no scorn of me, lest if thou make as tho' thou hearest not, I become like them that go down into the pit."[26] The poem itself also indicates the unpleasant qualities of scorn and being scorned: it suggests unreliable seekers of earthly power, since once Wolsey loses power "His suppliants scorn him, and his followers fly" (l. 112); and, of greater importance, it is something that one is blessed to escape from: "the virtues of a temp'rate prime / Bless [the good man] with an age exempt from scorn or crime" (ll. 291-292). In contrast to Democritus, the man who has properly searched and viewed the world, who has properly seen "the characters of mankind," also sees that they are not actors in a farce but in what may be called a divine comedy. Thus instead of scorn, "celestial wisdom calms the mind, / And makes the happiness she does not find" (ll. 367-368).

Johnson, then, does not use Democritus in anything like the way Juvenal does. He undercuts him from his introduction to his exit, subtly shows us that the pagan misrepresents man and cannot understand the Christian faith, hope and, among other traits, "love, which scarce collective man can fill" (l. 360), and he thereby makes clear that though Democritus' mirth may be "instructive" it instructs in a way different from what he intended: it shows us that harsh laughter is not a proper alternative, that the guided Christian audience will understand this and turn towards God, and that philosophy and scorn pale next to theology and love. In this case, it is clear, "An Answer from" the classical author has less power than that from the Christian.[27]

The Democritus passage and the conclusion may be analyzed in terms of the poem itself; but fully to appreciate Johnson's intention and achievement we must read Juvenal's Tenth Satire as well. What Johnson says about London is also true of The Vanity of Human Wishes: part of the "beauty of the Performance" consists in comparing the parent-poem with the Imitation.[28] And we should compare not only the superficial turns of a particular phrase but, among other matters, the attitude of the Imitator towards the parent-poem, the rhetorical situation of the respective speakers, and the peculiarities of the text the modern author used. In this way we might realize that there are few more versatile or original genres than the Augustan Imitation when written by poets like Pope or Johnson. Its earlier forms showed them some of its possibilities and limitations; they did not choose to translate, nor largely to ignore, nor to truncate their author; they chose, instead, to incorporate that author into their own structure, metaphor, and meaning, and thereby made an utterly new poem.

University of Wisconsin

NOTES

1. For relevant works on Augustan Imitation, see: William Francis Galloway, "English Adaptations of Roman Satire, 1660-1800" (unpublished Ph.D. Diss., University of Michigan, 1937); William K. Wimsatt, Jr., "Rhetoric and Poems: The Example of Pope," in English Institute Essays 1948 (New York, 1949), p. 183; Harold F. Brooks, "The 'Imitation' in English Poetry, Especially in Formal Satire, Before the Age of Pope," RES, XXV (1949), 124-140; Ian Jack, Augustan Satire (Oxford, 1952), pp. 97-114, 135-145; Reuben A. Brower, Alexander Pope: The Poetry of Allusion (Oxford, 1959); John Butt, ed., Alexander Pope: Imitations of Horace, The Twickenham Edition of the Poems of Alexander Pope, vol. IV (London, 1953), xxvi-xxx; Butt, "Johnson's Practice in the Poetical Imitation," in New Light on Dr. Johnson, ed. Frederick W. Hilles (New Haven, 1959), pp. 19-34; Mary Lascelles, "Johnson and Juvenal," ibid., pp. 35-55; G.K. Hunter, "The 'Romanticism' of Pope's Horace," EC, X (1960), 390-404; John M. Aden, "Pope and the Satiric Adversary," SEL, II (1962), 267-286; Aubrey L. Williams, "Pope and Horace: The Second Epistle of the Second Book," in Restoration and Eighteenth-Century Literature: Essays in Honor of Alan Dugald McKillop, ed. Carroll Camden (Chicago, 1963), pp. 309-321; Thomas E. Maresca, Pope's Horatian Poems (Columbus, Ohio, 1966); Howard D. Weinbrot, "Translation and Parody: Towards the Genealogy of the Augustan Imitation," ELH, XXXIII (1966), 434-447; Weinbrot, The Formal Strain: Studies in Augustan Imitation and Satire (Chicago, 1969); Leonard A. Moskovit, "Pope and the Tradition of the Neoclassical Imitation," SEL, VIII (1968), 445-462. The penultimate work cited above amplifies several of the points made in the present essay.

2. The Works of Mr. John Oldham, Together with his Remains (London, 1684); new pagination and title page after p. 148: Some New Pieces (London, 1684), sig. a$^v$ (italics and Roman type inverted in text).

3. For Cowley's Imitation, see Essays, Plays, and Sundry Verses, ed. A.R. Waller (Cambridge, 1906), pp. 412-413; and for the Latin and translation above, see Horace: The Odes and Epodes, Loeb Classical Library, trans. C.E. Bennett (Cambridge, Mass., 1934), p. 369.

4. For remarks regarding Rochester's Satyr, see: Johannes Prinz, John Wilmot Earl of Rochester (Leipzig, 1927), pp. 122-126; V. De Sola Pinto, Rochester: Portrait of a Restoration Poet (London, 1935), pp. 174-181; Francis Whitfield, Beast in View (Cambridge, Mass., 1936), pp. 50-54; S.F. Crocker, "Rochester's Satire Against Mankind: A Study of Certain Aspects of the Background," West Virginia University Studies, III (1937), 57-73; John F. Moore, "The Originality of Rochester's Satyr Against Mankind", PMLA, LVIII (1943), 393-401; Pinto, "John Wilmot, Earl of Rochester, and the Right Veine of Satire", in Essays and Studies by Members of the English Association, collected by Geoffrey Bullough, n.s., VI (London, 1953), 56-70; Thomas H. Fujimura, "Rochester's 'Satyr Against Mankind': An Analysis", SP, LV (1958), 576-590; C.F. Main, "The Right Vein of Rochester's Satyr," in Essays in Literary History Presented to J. Milton French, ed. Rudolf Kirk and C.F. Main (New Brunswick, N.J., 1960), pp. 93-112; Howard Erskine-Hill, "Rochester: Augustan or Explorer", in Renaissance and Modern Essays Presented to Vivian de Sola Pinto, ed. G.R. Hibbard (New York, 1966), pp. 51-64.

5. Lives of the English Poets, ed. G. Birkbeck Hill (Oxford, 1905), I, 226.

6. "The Originality of Rochester's Satyr Against Man", op. cit., 398-399.

7. Lives, I, 141.

8. Pope's earlier Imitations, The Imitations of the First Satire of the Second Book (Fortescue: 1733), and The Second Satire of the Second Book (Bethel: 1734), are "political" in an oblique rather than direct way, and they also turn to Horace as an authority of greater dignity than Pope. After the general election of 1734, "a short period of political calm set in," as Butt phrases it (Imitations, p. xxxvii), and Pope's poems refrain from primarily political concerns (though, again, they may be obliquely political, since the attack on Hervey-Sporus associates him with the Court). But by 1737, with the Opposition becoming more shrill, yet still unable to defeat Walpole, Pope begins to return to politics in earnest. In The Second Epistle of the Second Book (1737) Pope asserts his independence from the court, though in Fortescue he had, however jokingly, sought to please it; and in the Epistle to Augustus (1737) he savagely indicts the King and indirectly rejects Horace's authority. The political attacks rise in power

from The Sixth Epistle of the First Book (Murray: 1738) to The First Epistle of the First Book (Bolingbroke: 1738), and reach their peak in the Epilogue to the Satires (1738) where Pope overtly rejects Horace as a guide, associates him with servile court servants, shows the political and moral decay of England and, in a final note later appended to the Second Dialogue, indicates that the government was threatening his freedom. The final Dialogue looks forward to the terrors of the last book of the Dunciad where, Pope makes clear, Walpole-Palinurus at the helm of the ship of state continues to lead the nation into dullness and spiritual death. These political interests were developed fairly late in Pope's career. On 20 September 1723, Swift wrote to Pope praising the latter's good fortune: "you have no more to do with the constitution of Church and State than a Christian at Constantinople, and you are so much the wiser, and the happier because both partyes will approve your Poetry as long as you are known to be of neither" (The Correspondence of Alexander Pope, ed. George Sherburn [Oxford, 1956], II, 199).

9. The Literary Works of Matthew Prior, ed. H. Bunker Wright and Monroe K. Spears (Oxford, 1959), I, 140-41. Charles Kenneth Eves (Matthew Prior: Poet and Diplomatist [New York, 1939]) has shown much of Prior's intention in writing his English Ballad and, nevertheless, his great respect for Boileau. On September 13/23, 1695, Prior wrote to Tonson, saying: "You must print the French on one side, and with so much room between the stanzas as that the English may answer it, which you see is usually 12 lines, that is 3 alternate stanzas in English to one of 10 lines in French, tho sometimes it is but 8, and once but 4; I do not pretend it is an exact answer, nor do I care; 'tis only sense to those who understand the original" (Eves, p. 97). And in 1699, Eves reports: "with pardonable pride [Prior] cherished a compliment which Boileau made upon him [presumably in 1699]: 'Patience, I live amongst my savants, and Boileau says I have more genius than all the Academy'" (p. 137).

10. All quotations from London and the Vanity are from Samuel Johnson: Poems, The Yale Edition of the Works of Samuel Johnson, vol. VI, ed. E.L. McAdam, Jr., with George Milne (New Haven, 1964). For an important essay in the understanding of Juvenal's Third Satire, see William S. Anderson, "Studies in Book I of Juvenal", Yale Classical Studies, vol. XV, ed. Harry M. Hubbell (New Haven, 1957), pp. 56-68.

11. See <u>D. Junii Juvenalis et A. Persii Flacci Satyrae</u>, ed. Ludovicus Prateus (London, 1699) p. 62; Sir Robert Stapylton, <u>Juvenal's Sixteen Satyrs</u> (London, 1647), p. 46; Barton Holyday, <u>Decimus Junius Juvenalis, and Aulus Persius Flaccus</u> (Oxford, 1673), p. 43; John Dryden, <u>The Satires of Decimus Junius Juvenalis . . . Together with the Satires of Aulus Persius Flaccus</u> (London, 1693), p. 52. James Kinsley comments on these texts in <u>The Poems of John Dryden</u> (Oxford, 1958), IV, 2006.

12. <u>Juvenal and Persius</u>, Loeb Classical Library, trans. G.G. Ramsey (London, 1930), p. 57, 1. 322. All subsequent quotations are from this edition.

13. <u>D. Junii Juvenalis</u>, <u>op. cit.</u>, p. 62.

14. Quotations from the <u>Epistle to Augustus</u> are from Butt, <u>Imitations of Horace</u>, <u>op. cit.</u> For views similar to some of those expressed above, see Jay Arnold Levine, "Pope's <u>Epistle to Augustus</u>, lines 1-30", <u>SEL</u>, VII (1967), 427-451.

15. <u>Horace: Satires, Epistles, and Ars Poetica</u>, Loeb Classical Library, trans. H. Rushton Fairclough (Cambridge, Mass., 1926), pp. 397-399, 11. 18-21.

16. Pope himself glosses this line: "The Coronation of Henry the Eighth and Queen Anne Boleyn, in which the Playhouses vied with each other to represent all the pomp of a Coronation. In this noble contention, the Armour of one of the Kings of England was borrowed from the Tower, to dress the Champion" (<u>Imitations of Horace</u>, p. 223 n).

17. Swift uses this concept in his attack on Edward Young's <u>Love of Fame</u> (1725-28):

> For, such is good Example's Pow'r,
> It does its Office ev'ry Hour,
> Where <u>Governors</u> are good and wise;
> Or else the truest Maxim lyes:
> For this we know, all antient Sages
> Decree, that <u>ad exemplum Regis</u>,
> Thro' all the Realm his <u>Virtues</u> run,
> Rip'ning, and kindling like the Sun.

See *The Poems of Jonathan Swift*, ed. Harold Williams, 2nd ed. (Oxford, 1958), II, 391-392. See also Lyttelton's letter to Pope, 25 October 1738: "the Age is too far corrupted to Reform itself; it must be done by Those upon, or near the Throne, or not at all" (*Correspondence*, IV, 139).

18. In addition to the examples cited here, see those in Levine, "Pope's *Epistle to Augustus*," *op. cit.* Gibbon epitomizes this view, though with diction and tone more moderate than that of the writers involved in the political disputes of the 1730's. While Augustus restored "the dignity, he destroyed the independence of the senate. The principles of a free constitution are irrecoverably lost, when the legislative power is nominated by the executive." Gibbon then shows how Augustus "modelled and prepared" the senate, "displayed his patriotism, and disguised his ambition," and induced it to make him tyrant. "After a decent resistance the crafty tyrant submitted to the orders of the senate; and consented to receive the government of the provinces, and the general command of the Roman armies, under the well-known names of PROCUNSUL and IMPERATOR. But he would receive them only for ten years. Even before the expiration of that period, he hoped that the wounds of civil discord would be completely healed, and that the republic, restored to its pristine health and vigour, would no longer require the dangerous interposition of so extraordinary a magistrate. The memory of this comedy, repeated several times during the life of Augustus, was preserved to the last ages of the empre by the peculiar pomp with which the perpetual monarchs of Rome always solemnized the tenth year of their reign" (*The Decline and Fall of the Roman Empire*, ed. J.B. Bury [London, 1900], I, 60-61). For similar remarks by other historians of the period, see: Abbot de Vertot [Aubert de Vertot d'Aubeuf], *The History of the Revolutions that Happened in the Government of the Roman Republic* (London, 1721); Montesquieu, *Reflections on the Causes of the Grandeur and Declensions of the Romans* (London, 1734); Nathan Hooke, *The Roman History, From the Building of Rome to the Ruin of the Commonwealth*, 4 vols. (London, 1738, 1745, 1768, 1771); George Lord Lyttelton, *Observations on the Life of Cicero* (London, 1741); Abbe Bonot de Mably,*Observations on the Romans* (London, 1751); Thomas Blackwell, *Memoirs of the Court of Augustus*, 3 vols. (Edinburgh, 1753, 1755; London, 1763); Jean Baptiste Lewis Crevier, *The History of the Roman Empire, from Augustus to Constantine*, trans. John Mill (1755), 10 vols. (London, 1814); *A Short Review of Mr. Hooke's Observations concerning the Roman Senate, and the Character of Dionysius of Halicarnassus* (London, 1758); John Cleland, *The Woman of Honor*, 3 vols. (London, 1768), III, 55-56. These contemporary views are based upon observations and political theories in Polybius, Livy, Plutarch, and Tacitus, among others. I hope that the present essay (and similar work in progress) will lend further weight to the growing mistrust

of the first half of the eighteenth century as a positively "Augustan" age. In addition to Levine, cited above, see James W. Johnson, *The Formation of English Neo-Classical Thought* (Princeton, 1967); Howard Erskine-Hill, "Augustans on Augustanism in England, 1655-1759," *RMS*, XI (1967), 55-83; Ian Watt, ed., *The Augustan Age* (Greenwich, Conn., 1968), pp. 11-29.

19. "Observations on the Roman History," in *The Works of George Lord Lyttleton*, 3rd ed. (London, 1776), I, 39.

20. "Dialogues of the Dead. As published with Corrections, in 1765": "Dialogue IX," *ibid.*, II, 154-155.

21. *Ibid.*, p. 157.

22. Henry Gifford, "*The Vanity of Human Wishes*," *RES*, n.s., VI (1955), 158.

23. Contemporary readers were likely to be aware of the distinction between Democritus' and Johnson's views, as well as the poem's role as an Imitation with a particular sort of fictive setting. Here, for example, is Saint-Marc's reaction to Boileau's allusive method of adapting part of Juvenal's Sixth Satire in his own Tenth: "Ces vers ne sont en effet qu'une simple *allusion* à ceux de *Juvénal*, & ne les traduisent pas. J'ajoute que nôtre Auteur n'a pas dû rendre plus fidèlement le sens du Poëte Latin. Ce n'est pas lui qui parle, mais *Alcippe*, un homme du monde, qui doit avoir perdu de vuë depuis long temps les *Satires* de *Juvénal*, qu'il n'a vraisemblablement pas luës depuis ses Classes, & qui se ressouvenant en gros que ce Poëte est un Ecrivain fougueux & que la bile, que le domine, rend presque toujours outré, en cite les pensées conformément à l'idée qu'il s'est formée de l'Auteur." See *Oeuvres de M. Boileau Despréaux*, ed. M. de Saint-Marc (Paris, 1747), I, 168.

24. For an important essay regarding Juvenal's Tenth Satire, see D.E. Eicholz, "The Art of Juvenal and his Tenth Satire", *Greece and Rome*, 2nd series, III, (1956), 61-69.

25. Johnson might also have cited the Preface to *An Evening's Love* (1671), where Dryden distinguishes between comedy, which consists of "natural actions and characters," and farce, which "consists of forced humours, and unnatural events": *The Essays of John Dryden*, ed. W.P. Ker (Oxford, 1926), I, 135-137.

26. The King James version reads: "Unto thee will I cry, O LORD, my rock; be not silent to me: lest, *if* thou be silent to me, I become like them that go down into the pit."

27. This is also made clear in one of the familiar eighteenth-century comments regarding the conclusion of the poem: namely, that the pagan and Christian are in observable combat regarding the proper role of prayer and attitude towards Heaven. The pagan portrays an anthropomorphic god whom man can just as well do without; the Christian portrays a creative God to whom man turns because he cannot do without Him.

28. *The Letters of Samuel Johnson with Mrs. Thrale's Genuine Letters to Him*, ed. R.W. Chapman (Oxford, 1952), I, 11.

PARTICULAR AND GENERAL TRUTH:

SOME SPECULATIVE FOOTNOTES TO SCOTT ELLEDGE

By Jeffrey Hart

I

The eighteenth century discussion of generality and particularity had a variety of aspects and applications, depending upon whether one had in view a prescription for descriptive writing, selection of imagery, moral significance, character portrayal, or even painting and architecture. The descriptive writer, said Johnson, in the most inevitable quotation of all, must not "number the streaks of the tulip." Moving on, the moralist "must divest himself of the prejudices of his age and country; he must consider right and wrong in their abstracted and invariable state; he must disregard present laws and opinions, and rise to general and transcendental truths which will always be the same."

As for the portrayer of character, he should look to Shakespeare. "His persons act and speak by the influence of those passions and principles by which all minds are agitated, and the whole system of life is continued in motion. In the writings of other poets a character is too often an individual; in those of Shakespeare it is commonly a species."

And as long as we are citing Johnson, we should not neglect his friend and, in aesthetic theory, his willing disciple, Sir Joshua Reynolds. Contributing to Johnson's *Idler*, Reynolds denigrated the particularity of Dutch painting by comparing it with the universality of Italian: "The Italian attends only to the invariable, the great and general ideas which are fixed and inherent in universal nature; the Dutch, on the contrary, to literal truth and a minute exactness of detail, as I may say, of nature modified by accident. The attention to these petty peculiarities is the very cause of this naturalness so much admired in Dutch pictures, which, if we suppose it to be a beauty, is certainly of a lower order" (No. 79). Three numbers later, Reynolds returned to the theme and, suitably, generalized it: "In consequence of having seen many [individuals of the same species] the power is acquired . . . of distinguishing between accidental blemishes and excrescences which are continually varying the surface of nature's works, and the invariable general form which nature most frequently produces, and always seems to intend in her productions."

As far as social role is concerned, the idea of universality embodied itself in the normative idea of decorum -- in, for example, Pope's assumptions about the typical in social character: deviation from the norm is a cause of merriment, a ludicrous perversion of that clear, unchanged, and universal light. The poet who wanted to sink in poetry should, Pope ironically advised, "affect the marvellous" by drawing "Achilles with the patience of Job; a Prince talking like a Jack Pudding; a Maid of Honour selling bargains; a footman speaking like a philosopher; and a fine gentleman like a scholar."

Joseph Addison saw that architecture, too, exhibited analogues of the universal and the particular. The Pantheon, he thought, possessed grandeur because of the sweep and simplicity of its elements, whereas the detail, the particularity, of a gothic cathedral, its redundancy of smaller ornament, dividing and scattering the attention, appeared "but a confusion."

To be sure, all of these writers made contradictory statements or made statements which, if not contradictory, at least were expressive of an opposite tendency. Johnson leaned toward generality, and Cowley's labored particularity barred him from the very highest achievement; still it was Thomson's particularity that made The Seasons notable. Reynolds' theory pointed to Raphael, but he confessed that he preferred Michaelangelo. Pope's satire frequently depended upon the universality of norms, but he also praised Homer for his minutely observed particulars, and the Dunciad arrives at universals -- if it does arrive at them -- by way of a sandstorm of particulars.

Still, the question is one of emphasis; and the weight of utterance, as well as the weight of practice, in these writers is on the side of universality as against particularity. Nature's light is clear, unchanging, and universal; genuine truths obtain from China to Peru; and the important things are always the same.

But from our own point of view the question naturally arises of why this issue was so insisted upon. The question of generality and particularity does not seem central to the discussions of Renaissance rhetoricians, and we do not hear much about it from the principal writers of the age of Elizabeth. It does not preoccupy the seventeenth century. Why, then, does it become central for the eighteenth century, and what is the meaning of its centrality?

II

The first thing to be observed is that the issue of the universal and the particular has been, if not a perennial issue, at least a periodic one. For the historian, its interest may reside in its very periodicity: in the conditions which make it a pressing, a central issue.

First of all, when has the issue of generality and particularity become central? Plato raised it in the most thoroughgoing way imaginable, and he drove his solution to the limit of the dialectic. What is real *is* the idea -- not the individual, as Johnson would put it, but the species. The quest for the historical Socrates has yet to be rewarded with success, but the Socrates of the Dialogues, at least, is the first Realist. Emphasizing the mutability doctrine of Heraclitus, the Sophists had rendered knowledge impossible: "Into the same river no man ever plunges twice: the river has changed, and he himself has changed." To this Socrates, and Plato with him, answer: "The river passes, the man changes, but humanity and fluidity abide. The individual is changing and deceptive; the Universal is unchanging and trustworthy." Thus, under the special, but recurring, circumstances of fourth century Athens, metaphysics was born. Aristotle, while muting the oppositions of Plato's dialectic, made the general and the particular central to his definition of poetry. He did not say, as Auden once did, that poetry is the form in which the lines go only part of the way across the page, instead of all the way. He said that poetry expressed the idea of the thing, the probability, whereas history recorded the accidental -- the ragged, improbable particulars. Poetry -- truth -- was the intention toward which history aspired, only to be frustrated by the incalculable.

Again and again the issue comes forward, only to recede again. In their rhetorical advice Quintilian and Longinus reflect different aesthetic emphases, though neither moves to the philosophical depths. Quintilian urged the effectiveness of descriptive particulars:

> The mere statement that the town was stormed, while no doubt it embraces all that such a calamity involves, has all the curtness of a despatch, and fails to penetrate the emotions of the hearer. But if we expand all that the word "stormed" includes, we shall see the flames pouring from the house and temple . . . we shall behold some in doubt whither to fly, others clinging to their nearest and dearest in one embrace . . . Then will come the pillage of treasure sacred and profane . . . the victors fighting over the richest of the spoil.

Longinus, on the other hand, urges the opposite tendency and denigrates the "triviality" of detail, which is apt to "disfigure sublimity." In Chapter 43 of the *Peri Hypsous*, Longinus ridicules a long passage of detailed description, and concludes that it might have been more effectively rendered "in broad outline."

The dialectical problem of the particular and the general was posed sharply once again during the later middle ages by the scholastic philosophers. Augustine's metaphysics had had Platonism as its point of departure, and it was by way of Augustine that metaphysics passed to the scholastics: though the intractable particularity of Christianity -- the scandal of its particular revelation, and of its belief in a particular incarnation -- prevented the scholastics from following the Platonic logic of the universal to its obvious conclusion: the assertion of one real, all-pervading abstract principle, the Idea of the Cosmos: pantheism, Spinoza. Yet against the scholastic Realist position, there arose a clearly formulated nominalism, or doctrine of particularity. As an example of extreme nominalism, we may take Roscellinus, who died about 1105. He maintained that the universal was merely a manner of speaking, a convenient fiction -- in the end, an empty breath, "*non nisi flatus vocis*." This seems downright, but upon reflection it runs into difficulties. Roscellinus' view that all the things we call *horse* have nothing in common except the name, that the name is a mere convenience of notation as it were, runs into the natural question: why do we call *these* horses and *those* cows? Is there no *quiddity*, no limit beyond which a thing is something else? And can we consider a mere empty breath that which gives a set of particulars their common character? If extreme realism seems to common sense to be chimerical, extreme nominalism seems upon reflection to be absurd.

Until the end of the seventeenth century the issue, as it were, slept; or perhaps it would be better to say that it was in abeyance because nominalism so completely dominated the field -- from Rabelais' thesaurus of particulars and Montaigne's *Essays* to Bacon's empiricism and the particularities of seventeenth century poetic style which Johnson was to find so unsatisfactory in Donne and Cowley. Nominalism, at least in its heroic phase, had about it an atmosphere of liberation, a sense of freedom gained from the structure -- felt to be excessive -- of medieval rationalism and realism. The Platonic tradition was either mainly literary, as at Florence, or underground, as at seventeenth century Cambridge.

At the end of the seventeenth century the issue of the universal and the particular became serious again, moved back to the center of the stage. But why? Heretofore, most of the answers have been couched in terms of "influence." Shaftesbury, it has been pointed out, drew upon both Plato and Aristotle and arrived at conclusions much like Johnson's about the universal and the particular:

> Now the variety of Nature is such as to distinguish everything she forms, by a <u>peculiar</u> original Character; which, if strictly observ'd, will make the Subject appear unlike to anything extant in the World besides. But this Effect the good Poet and Painter seeks industriously to prevent. They hate <u>Minuteness</u>, and are afraid of <u>Singularity</u>; which would make their Images, or Characters, appear capricious and fantastical. The mere Face-Painter, indeed, has little in common with the Poet; but, like the mere Historian, copies what he sees, and minutely traces every Feature, and odd Mark. 'Tis otherwise with the Men of Invention and Design. 'Tis from <u>many</u> Objects of Nature, and not from a Particular one, that those Genius's form the Idea of their Work.

In his <u>Reflections . . . upon . . . An Essay Upon Criticism</u> John Dennis espoused a similar view:

> [Horace] makes it clear as the Sun, what it is to follow Nature in giving a draught of human Life, and of the manners of Men, and that is not to draw after particular Men, who are but Copies and imperfect Copies of the great universal Pattern; but to consult that innate Original, and that universal Idea, which the Creator has fix'd in the minds of ev'ry reasonable Creature.

It is unlikely then, that anyone will question Scott Elledge's conclusion: "we must suppose that, derivative or first hand, the teachings of Plato were just as much a part of Dr. Johnson's thinking as they had been of every critic's since the Renaissance."

But this does not explain why the question of the particular and the universal came to the fore only at the end of the seventeenth century. If Plato, Aristotle, and indeed the Schoolmen could provide a source "since the Renaissance," why was it that we hear so little about the matter during the seventeenth century, and so much during the eighteenth?

In his seminal article on the subject, Scott Elledge offers an ingenious and important argument from circumstance. The issue of the universal and the particular became current only after 1676, when Dryden, having read for the first time Boileau's Traité du Sublime ou du Merveilleux dans le Discours Traduit du Grec de Longin, introduced the question of the Sublime into English criticism with the announcement in his "Apology for Heroic Poetry" that Longinus was "after Aristotle the greatest critic amongst the Greeks." The influence of Longinus, Elledge shows convincingly, greatly reinforced the argument against particularity. Sublimity and grandeur, so the argument ran, "are nearly synonymous; one quality common to all things sublime in nature or art is large size, and what distinguishes the experience of anything sublime is that the mind, or soul, or imagination is filled to overflowing. This basic assumption would naturally lead to the notion that smallness, even when it is only a characteristic of parts which together make a grand whole, will work against sublimity." "Triviality of expression," urged Longinus in the Peri Hupsous, is "apt to disfigure sublimity." And he witheringly attacks a descriptive passage in Theopompus, concluding: "he might have described the scene in broad outline."

After the initial impetus provided by Dryden, Longinus' treatise on the sublime became the point of departure for the critical discussion so exhaustively described by Samuel Monk; and throughout the discussion an affirmation of sublimity militated against particularity. In The Grounds of Criticism in Poetry, for example, John Dennis most frequently chose as preeminent instances of the sublime those passages from Paradise Lost which are most free of detail. In Addison's opinion, the detail of a Gothic cathedral made it inferior in sublimity to the Pantheon, even though the cathedral was much larger. In his Essay on the Sublime (1747), John Baillie stressed the quality of uniformity as necessary to the sublime: "where this Uniformity is wanting, the Mind must run from Object to Object, and never get a full and compleat Prospect. Thus instead of having one large and grand Idea, a thousand little ones are shuffled in. Here the Magnitude of the Scene is entirely broke, and consequently the noble Pride and sublime Sensation destroy'd." As Elledge concludes: "All the implications about the dependence of sublimity upon general impression as they are made by Longinus, Dennis, Addison, and Baillie became explicit in Burke's Philosophical Enquiry into the Origin of Our Ideas of the Sublime and the Beautiful" -- a book thoroughly familiar to both Johnson and Reynolds. And indeed Johnson does connect grandeur with generality in his famous judgment of Abraham Cowley:

> Great thoughts are always general, and consist in
> propositions not limited by exceptions, and
> in descriptions not descending to minuteness.
>
> The fault of Cowley, and perhaps of all of the
> writers of the metaphysical race, is that of
> pursuing his thoughts to their last ramifica-
> tions, by which he loses the grandeur of gener-
> ality; . . . all the power of description is
> destroyed by a scrupulous enumeration.

To Elledge's thesis, then -- that the neoclassical affirmation of generality received powerful reinforcement from the discussion of the sublime -- only one reservation need here be urged. Neither Johnson nor Reynolds, while urging the grandeur of the general, showed comparable enthusiasm for those other hallmarks of the sublime as conceived during the eighteenth century: obscurity, infinity, darkness, passion, the rhapsodic. Indeed, their critical temper resolutely resisted these qualities. As Wimsatt remarks about Johnson's attitude toward the sublime: "Johnson's surrender to the sublime . . . was limited by his shrewd and orthodox realization that it was in effect a new form of religion -- rhapsodic and worshipful of outdoor nature." Indeed a surrender so limited would seem to be inappropriately described as a surrender; and if the authority of Longinus, reinforced by Dryden, and transmitted by continuous discussion, encouraged the affirmation of generality by Johnson and Renyolds, it nevertheless did not encourage them to embrace the other Longinian qualities.

Numerous sources, then, have plausibly been suggested for the neoclassical universal: Plato, Aristotle, Augustine, the Schoolmen, Longinus, even the Cartesian and geometric standards of clear reason and the Newtonian concept of a universe governed by uniform laws of motion. But if such sources indubitably were available, why were they drawn upon in just this way? Since they are always, more or less, thus available, why should we find a special emphasis upon generality coming to the fore among certain important eighteenth-century critics and writers? Elledge proposes a historical answer: the authority of Dryden launched Longinus upon his eighteenth-century career. But this still leaves the question open; and I would like to offer, in addition, a more speculative hypothesis.

### III

I think it will be agreed that all meaning is a function of relation. Things are good, bad, high, low, valuable, cheap, hot, cold, large, small, sweet, sour, important, unimportant, only in relationship to something else. To mean is to signify, to make a sign pointing away from the object and toward other objects with which it stands in "significant" relation. The idea "father" is intelligible only in relation to "mother" and "offspring." The idea of a "mountain" is intelligible only in relation to "earth" and "valley." A thing stripped of all relations would not mean, it would merely be. A universe composed of completely unrelated objects would be devoid of meaning; and it would be wordless, since words are a way of making connections among things. (To be sure, such a universe is impossible to imagine, since objects must have at least "existence" in common; and the poet laureate of such a universe could utter two words: They Are.) Yet such lack of relation is the terminus toward which nominalism tends; as particulars detach themselves from relations we move toward the condition of being able to say only that they are.

At the beginning of <u>Bleak House</u>, for example, Dickens introduces us to just such a world of isolated and therefore meaningless particulars. The fog is pervasive, concealing relations, raising the question, indeed, of whether relations, and therefore meaning, exist:

> "Fog creeping into the cabooses of collier-brigs; fog lying out on the yards, and hovering in the rigging of the great ships; fog drooping on the gunwales of barges and small boats. Fog in the eyes and throats of ancient Greenwich pensioners, wheezing by the firesides of their wards; fog in the stem and bowl of the afternoon pipe of the wrathful skipper, down in his close cabin; fog cruelly pinching the toes and fingers of his shivering little 'prentice boy on deck."

In his remarkable book on Dickens, J. Hillis Miller makes the appropriate comment on the meaning of this passage:

> "These objects and people are more separated by the fog than linked by it. The fog, a fog that is both a physical mist and a spiritual blindness, forms an opaque barrier between one place and any other. The wrathful skipper is indifferent to the suffering of the 'prentice boy on deck; neither of them is aware of the ancient Greenwich pensioners; and the narrator too is at a distance from any of these people or objects. They are seen from the outside. What is seen forms a <u>tableau</u> in which everything is present at once in a pell-mell disorder, like the cows and people in a painting by Chagall. Things are visible, outlined in the fog, but nothing is related to anything else. Each new object is simply added to the others in a succession which makes more and more obvious their disconnection. Each fragmentary glimpse is like a momentary illumination from one direction of an unknown object. The sum of all these glimpses cannot be added up to make a

> coherent three-dimensional shape . . . [The] spectator ends, it may be, like Baudelaire at the sight of seven identical old men appearing one by one out of the fog, 'blessé par le mystère et par l'absurdité.' Is it a 'mystery,' or is it merely an 'absurdity.' Do these appearances hide a secret order and meaning or are they indeed a chaos?"

Until we can establish relations, there is no meaning.

Now since poetry is centrally concerned with meaning, it is centrally concerned with the establishing of relations; which is why metaphor is so important to poetry, though metaphor is of course not the only way of bringing relations to light. Sometimes, as in metaphysical poetry, relatedness is typically under great stress. The premise is particularity, a circumstance in which all coherence is gone. The heterogeneity to be organized, if possible, is of an extreme character: a "bracelet of bright hair about the bone." These observations point, I think, to the meaning of the metaphysical style. As a rhetorical pattern it strives characteristically to establish relations within a circumstance of extreme heterogeneity. It moves dialectically. Lovers and compasses become lover-compasses. Lovers and saints become saintly lovers. If metaphor is one way of perceiving meaning through a perception of relationships, the conceit is merely a metaphor operating under the apprehension of extreme particularity; and I think we may entertain the suggestion, at least, that the metaphysical conceit expresses the discontent of the seventeenth-century poetic imagination with Renaissance nominalism. Better a well wrought urn than the half-acre tombs of Rabelais and Montaigne.

But if the conceit is one way of insisting upon the necessity of meaning and relation as well as upon the radical difficulty of apprehending them, the neoclassical universal has a rather different bearing. The universal testifies to relations which have already been discovered, which are "everywhere the same." It testifies to meanings which are available not only to an individual act of vision -- as in the metaphysical conceit -- but which are available to "mankind." Those relations have been envisioned and corporately agreed upon; and indeed the universal is corporate rather than individualistic, for it looks to what men have in common rather than to what separates them. The cultural circumstance for which the universal is the appropriate rhetorical gesture is one in which meaning is felt to be objective and generally available. It resides in permanent relations which may be discerned because they are in fact <u>there</u>.

But as everyone has recognized, the issue in the eighteenth century is not a simple one. Those relations are there, but they are not entirely agreed upon; the focus wavers; the assertion of generality by Johnson and Reynolds both is and is not assured; it has about it the look of a position under attack and therefore insisted upon. Johnson recommends generality and judges Cowley adversely; but he praises the particularity of Thomson's Seasons in terms which echo Joseph Warton's Essay on the Writings and Genius of Pope. There was "mankind" from China to Peru; but there was also individual biography; and there was the particularity of Richardson.

And again, as everyone knows, the eighteenth century exhibited a vast intensification of interest in and affirmation of particularity. Ian Watt has shown that particularity is the distinguishing quality of the new, the novel genre of the century -- the novel: particularity of time, of place, and of character. And the interest of such particularism is not the corporate interest in what men have in common, but an individualistic interest in the ways in which they differ, in their variations. "The growth of the novel, therefore," as Chesterton said, "must not be too easily called an increase in the interest in humanity. It is an increase in the interest in the things in which men differ; much fuller and finer work had been done before about the things in which they agree."

And if an affirmation of generality links the theoretical pronouncements of Johnson and Reynolds with those of Pope, Addison, Baillie and Shaftesbury, and beyond them with the Schoolmen, with Plato and Aristotle, there also existed in eighteenth-century aesthetic theory a strong current of particularity. Kames urged the avoidance of "abstract and general terms" and thought that the life of poetry resided in "particular objects." Ogilvie, Campbell, and Blair provided a similar emphasis. Hume's epistemology is surely an ultimate in nominalism, and Adam Smith projected an individualist economics. If we can locate Johnson and Reynolds in a tradition of corporate universalists stretching back to Plato and Aristotle, the pedigree of these eighteenth century nominalists and particularists is equally venerable, stretching back through Locke, Hobbes and the empirical tradition to the ancient atomists. Indeed, though the tradition associated with Pope and Johnson produced the best poetry of the century, and set the literary tone, the particularist and nominalist position doubtless reflected the main cultural and social tendency. "Modern scholars and critics," Paul Fussell notes, "are perceiving increasingly that the Augustan humanists, far from being 'representative' of the general tendencies of their time, constitute actually an intensely anachronistic and reactionary response to the eighteenth century. Their rhetorical careers conduct a more or less constant warfare with the 'official' assumptions of their age, assumptions held by most of their contemporaries."

The speculative conclusion I wish to urge, therefore, may be stated as follows: The affirmation of generality during the eighteenth century may be read as an appeal to community and to shared meaning as against an increasingly powerful individualism expressing itself through an aesthetics -- as well as an epistemology and an economics -- of particularity.

## IV

The movement toward particularity, however, poses what might be called the classic problem of modernity. If meaning and relation are not <u>there</u>, perceived as agreed upon generalizations, then the individual must make those meanings for himself: <u>create</u> the relations, create the meaning. The movement toward particularity and away from generality is inevitably a movement toward individuality and the subjectivization of meaning. It envisages, as a terminus, the extreme individualism of the existentialist who creates, in complete freedom, his "project."

But that is not, of course, the end of the story. On the last page of his indispensable essay, Scott Elledge refers to the "extreme particularity which the twentieth century now takes without question." He cites T.S. Eliot's adverse judgment of Milton for not conveying "the feeling of being in a particular place at a particular time." And Elledge is surely right to point to the extreme particularity of the classic modern authors. <u>The Waste Land</u> consists, avowedly and intentionally, of "fragments." And other modern works seem, often, like cosmic grab-bags full of nothing but particulars. Think of <u>Ulysses</u>, or Pound's <u>Cantos</u>: the details are -- and are meant to be -- overwhelming. The <u>Cantos</u> may be the most particularistic book ever written.

But, again, this is not the whole story. Beneath the overwhelming particularity -- intended to reflect the extreme heterogeneity of modern experience -- the deep movement may be the groundswell of generality. Cabestan's twelfth-century heart may be in the dish, in Canto IV, and Old Vidal may dress himself in skins to pursue his love, only to be set upon by wolves; but both incarnate a pattern, adumbrated in myth: they incarnate the stories of Procne and Tereus, Actaeon and Artemis. Pound, the supreme individualist of twentieth-century literature, has in fact written an epic poem about the particular and the universal, about how history is the recurrence of pattern, of recurrence though always with "a difference." The act of reading the <u>Cantos</u>, like the act of reading <u>Ulysses</u> or <u>Finnegan's Wake</u>, involves a transcendence of the merely particular and a recovery of relation, pattern, meaning.

Somewhere Cassirer remarks that cultural periods are distinguished not by the answers they give but by the questions they ask. Surely the characteristic question asked by our time is: What is the meaning of history? Where is the pattern of relations amongst all these particulars? Where, that is, do we look for the necessary generalization? Sometimes, as in Marx, Spengler, or Toynbee, it is a _telos_, a goal toward which history moves. Joyce employs classical epic and myth to generalize his moment. Jung has his archetypes. Yeats invents his own system of relations. Eliot sees the pattern as organized by the still point, the moment in and out of time. There thus exists abundant evidence that the modern consciousness is impatient with an extreme nominalism.

Dartmouth College

THE LITERATURE OF NEOCLASSICISM, 1920-1968:  A BIBLIOGRAPHY

THE LITERATURE OF NEOCLASSICISM, 1920-1968: A BIBLIOGRAPHY

Paul J. Korshin

An earlier version of this bibliography was distributed to participants in Conference 28 at the 1967 MLA Annual Meeting. Entitled "A Checklist of Recent 'Augustan' Literature, 1950-1967," the small number of copies was soon exhausted; it contained 194 items, of which about 15 percent were dissertations. This present bibliography attempts to do somewhat more than its smaller predecessor, by carrying the _terminus_ a _quo_ back to the earlier years of this century, and by including titles outside of the strict confines of literature. Clearly, however, it is impossible for a listing of published material dealing with Neoclassicism to be all-inclusive. A complete listing of every work during this period which mentions or refers to Neoclassicism, the Augustan age or Augustanism, and the other related concepts used by scholars of the eighteenth century, would have to be enormous and would ultimately be trivial. Thus I have tried to collect a reference to every substantial utterance, and to most of the important peripheral discussions, concerning the Neoclassical period, its intellectual background, and its major authors. It seemed best to exclude dissertations, unless published at least in part, since it is difficult to find every American or foreign thesis dealing with Neoclassicism. Even without this very numerous accumulation, this bibliography includes nearly 900 items published since 1920.

It is almost a commonplace for prefaces to bibliographical compilations to assert that interest in the subject at hand has accelerated ever more rapidly in recent years. But this is not specifically the case with writings dealing with Neoclassicism and the literary theory concerning it: it seems, rather, that critical interest in this topic has, with certain interesting fluctuations, maintained a constant flow of several dozen items per year for the last few decades. Hence such a listing as this may be useful to students of the field for a few years, unless a sudden deluge brings it to rapid obsolescence. I regret that it cannot be a more exhaustive listing than it is, but even such polymathic bibliographers as Maittaire and Fabricius overlooked some books. Nor can the work of one individual be perfect, so I apologize for any incidental lacunae or errors. I hope, however, as others doubtless do, that in the near future it may be possible to publish a more complete bibliography of Neoclassical scholarship, tracing the concept back into the nineteenth century, annotating items where necessary, and including the immensely valuable reviews of scholarly books in the last fifty years.

|      |                                                                                            | Page |
|------|--------------------------------------------------------------------------------------------|------|
| I.   | Bibliography                                                                               | 87   |
| II.  | General Background: Intellectual History, Culture, Taste, and Science                      | 88   |
| III. | Literary History and Criticism: Literary Theory, Aesthetics, and Stylistics                | 101  |
| IV.  | Poetics                                                                                    | 120  |
| V.   | The Other Genres: Fiction, Drama, Satire, etc.                                             | 129  |
| VI.  | Literature and the Other Arts                                                              | 133  |
| VII. | The Arts                                                                                   | 135  |
| VIII.| Texts and Anthologies                                                                      | 138  |
| IX.  | Individual Authors                                                                         | 141  |
| X.   | Continental Background                                                                     | 155  |

Abbreviations for periodical titles, where used, conform to those given in the MLA International Bibliography.

## I. Bibliography

Brown, Huntington. "The Classical Tradition in English Literature: A Bibliography," *Harvard Studies and Notes in Philology and Literature*, XVIII (1935), 7-16.

Cooper, Lane and Alfred Gudeman. *A Bibliography of the "Poetics" of Aristotle*. (Cornell Studies in English, XI.) New Haven: Yale Univ. Press; London: Oxford Univ. Press, 1928.

Cordasco, Francesco. *A Register of 18th Century Bibliographies and References: A Chronological Quarter-Century Survey Relating to English Literature, Booksellers, Newspapers, Periodicals, Printing and Publishing; Aesthetics, Art, and Music; Economics, History and Science*. Chicago: V. Giorgio; Milano: Sansoni; Roma: Valecchi; Paris: Alterto Tallone, 1950.

Draper, John W. *Eighteenth Century English Aesthetics: A Bibliography*. ("Anglistische Forschungen," Heft 71.) Heidelberg: Carl Winter, 1931.

Hammond, William A. *A Bibliography of Aesthetics and of the Philosophy of the Fine Arts from 1900 to 1932*. New York: Longmans Green, 1933.

Herrick, Marvin T. "A Supplement to Cooper and Gudeman's Bibliography of the *Poetics* of Aristotle," *American Journal of Philology*, LII (1931), 168-174.

Ogden, Henry V.S. and Margaret Ogden. "A Bibliography of Seventeenth-Century Writings on the Pictorial Arts in English," *Art Bulletin*, XXIX (1947), 196-201.

Pargellis, Stanley, and D.J. Medley (eds.). *Bibliography of British History: The Eighteenth Century, 1714-1789*. Issued under the direction of the American Historical Association and the Royal Historical Society of Great Britain. Oxford: Clarendon Press, 1951.

Templeman, William D. "Contribution to the Bibliography of Eighteenth-Century Aesthetics," *MP*, XXX (1933), 309-316.

Tobin, James E. *Eighteenth Century English Literature and its Cultural Background. A Bibliography*. New York: Fordham University Press, 1939.

Vowles, Richard B. "Dramatic Theory: A Bibliography," <u>Bulletin of the New York Public Library</u>, LIX (1955), 412-428, 464-482, 525-534, 578-585.

Wellek, René. "Studies in Eighteenth-Century English Literature, 1938-1945," <u>Erasmus</u>, I (1947), 658-676.

## II. General Background: Intellectual History, Culture, Taste, and Science

Allen, Arthur Bruce. <u>Eighteenth-Century England: The Complete Background Book</u>. London: Rockliff, 1955.

Allen, B. Sprague. <u>Tides in English Taste (1619-1800). A Background for the Study of Literature</u>. 2 vols. Cambridge, Mass.: Harvard University Press, 1937.

Allen, Robert J. <u>The Clubs of Augustan London</u>. (Harvard Studies in English, VII.) Cambridge, Mass.: Harvard University Press, 1933.

Alloway, Lawrence. "Eighteenth Century Taste," <u>Listener</u>, LIV (8 December 1955), 1008.

Appleton, William W. <u>Cycle of Cathay: The Chinese Vogue in England during the Seventeenth and Eighteenth Centuries</u>. New York: Columbia Univ. Press, 1951.

Armytage, Walter Harry Green. <u>Heavens Below: Utopian Experiment in England, 1560-1960</u>. London: Routledge; Toronto: University of Toronto Press, 1961.

Aronson, A. "The Anatomy of Taste: A Note on Eighteenth Century Periodical Literature," <u>MLN</u>, LXI (1946), 228-236.

Ashley, Maurice. <u>England in the Seventeenth Century (1603-1714)</u>. (The Pelican History of England, 6.) London and Baltimore: Penguin Books, 1952.

Bahlman, Dudley W.R. <u>The Moral Revolution of 1688</u>. (Wallace Notestein Essays, No. 2. Yale Historical Publications, Vol. 38.) New Haven: Yale University Press, 1957.

Balz, Albert G.A. <u>Descartes and the Modern Mind</u>. New Haven: Yale University Press; London: Cumberlege, 1952.

Barnes, Harry Elmer. *A History of Historical Writing*. Norman: University of Oklahoma Press, 1937.

Becker, Carl L. *The Heavenly City of the Eighteenth-Century Philosophers*. (The Storrs Lectures.) New Haven: Yale University Press, 1932.

Beljame, Alexandre. *Men of Letters and the English Public in the Eighteenth Century, 1660-1744: Dryden, Addison, Pope*. London: Kegan Paul, 1948.

Beloff, Max. *The Age of Absolutism, 1660-1815*. London: Hutchinson's University Library, 1954.

Bethell, S.L. *The Cultural Revolution of the Seventeenth Century*. London: Dennis Pobson, 1951.

Bloom, Edward A. "'Labors of the Learned:' Neo-Classic Book Reviewing Aims and Techniques," *SP*, LIV (1957), 537-563.

Bloom, Edward A. "Neoclassic 'Paperwars' for a Free Press," *MLR*, LVI (1961), 481-496.

Bloomfield, Paul. *Uncommon People: A Study of England's Elite*. London: Hamilton, 1955.

Bolgar, Robert R. *The Classical Heritage and Its Beneficiaries*. Cambridge: Cambridge University Press, 1954.

Bracey, Robert. *Eighteenth Century Studies*. Oxford: Blackwell, 1925.

Brandenburg, Alice S. "English Education and Neo-Classical Taste in the Eighteenth Century," *MLQ*, VIII (1947), 174-193.

Brauer, Jerald C. "Puritan Mysticism and the Development of Liberalism," *Church History*, XIX (1950), 151-170.

Brauer, George C. Jr. "Good Breeding in the Eighteenth Century," *University of Texas Studies in English*, XXXII (1953), 25-44.

Bredvold, Louis I. *The Brave New World of the Enlightenment*. Ann Arbor: University of Michigan Press, 1961.

Bredvold, Louis I. "The Invention of the Ethical Calculus," The Seventeenth Century: Studies in the History of English Thought and Literature from Bacon to Pope, by Richard Foster Jones and Others Writing in his Honor, (Stanford: Stanford University Press, 1951), 165-180.

Bredvold, Louis I. The Natural History of Sensibility. Detroit: Wayne State University Press, 1962.

Bredvold, Louis I. "Some Basic Issues of the Eighteenth Century," Michigan Alumnus Quarterly Review, LXIV (1957), 45-54.

Bréhier, Emile. Histoire de la Philosophie. Tome II, La Philosophie Moderne. i, "Le dix-septième siècle." ii, "Le dix-huitième siècle." Paris; Alcan: 1929-30.

Bronson, Bertrand H. Printing as an Index of Taste in Eighteenth Century England. New York: New York Public Library, 1958.

Bush, Douglas. Science and English Poetry. New York: Oxford University Press, 1950.

Butt, John. The Augustan Age. London: Hutchinson, 1950.

Carré, Meyrick H. "The Old Order and the New: The Intellectual Revolution of the Seventeenth Century," History Today, V (1955), 153-161.

Carré, Meyrick H. Phases of Thought in England. Oxford: Clarendon Press; New York: Oxford University Press, 1949.

Carré, Meyrick H. "Robert Boyle and English Thought," History Today, VII (1957), 322-327.

Cassirer, Ernst. The Philosophy of the Enlightenment. Trans. Fritz C.A. Koelln and James P. Pettegrove. Princeton: Princeton University Press, 1951.

Cassirer, Ernst. The Platonic Renaissance in England. Trans. James P. Pettegrove. London: Nelson; Austin: University of Texas Press, 1953.

Clark, Kenneth. The Gothic Revival, An Essay in the History of Taste. London: Constable & Co., 1928.

Clark, Sir George Norman. *War and Society in the Seventeenth Century*. (Wiles Lectures, 1956.) Cambridge: Cambridge University Press, 1958.

Cragg, Gerald R. *From Puritanism to the Age of Reason: A Study of Changes in Religious Thought within the Church of England, 1660-1700*. Cambridge: Cambridge University Press, 1950.

Cragg, Gerald R. *Reason and Authority in the Eighteenth Century*. Cambridge: Cambridge University Press, 1964.

Cragg, Gerald R. *Puritanism in the Period of the Great Persecution, 1660-1688*. New York: Cambridge University Press, 1957.

Cragg, Gerald R. *The Church and the Age of Reason, 1648-1789*. (Pelican History of the Church, 4.) Harmondsworth: Penguin Books, 1960.

Crane, Ronald S. "Anglican Apologetics and the Idea of Progress, 1699-1745," *MP*, XXXI (1934), 273-306, 349-382.

Crane, Ronald S. "Interpretation of Texts and the History of Ideas," *College English*, II (1941), 755-765.

Crane, Ronald S. "Literature, Philosophy, and the History of Ideas," *MP*, LII (1954), 73-83.

Crane, Ronald S. "Suggestions Toward a Genealogy of the 'Man of Feeling'," *ELH*, I (1934), 205-230.

Crum, Ralph B. *Scientific Thought in Poetry*. New York: Columbia University Press, 1931.

Das, Praphulla Kumar. *Evidences of a Growing Taste for Nature in the Age of Pope*. Calcutta: Calcutta University Press, 1928.

Davies, G.C.B. "The Early Evangelicals," *Church Quarterly Review*, CLV (1954), 121-130.

De Maar, Hargo G. *A History of Modern English Romanticism, Vol. I: Elizabethan and Modern Romanticism in the Eighteenth Century*. London: Humphrey Milford, Oxford University Press, 1924.

Douglas, David C. "The Development of English Medieval Scholarship Between 1660 and 1730," *Transactions of the Royal Historical Society*, XXI (1939), 21-39.

Douglas, David C. *English Scholars*. London: Cape, 1939.

Dyson, H.V.D., and Butt, John. *Augustans and Romantics, 1689-1830. With Chapters on Art, Economics and Philosophy by Geoffrey Webb, F.J. Fisher and H.A. Hodges*. (Introductions to Literature, ed. Bonamy Dobree, Vol. III.) London: Cresset Press, 1940. 3rd ed., rev., London: Cresset Press, 1961.

Elliott-Binns, L.E. *The Early Evangelicals: A Religious and Social Study*. London: Lutterworth Press; Greenwich, Conn.: Seaburg Press, 1953.

Evans, B. Ifor. *Literature and Science*. London: Allen and Unwin, 1954.

Foxon, David. "Libertine Literature in England, 1660-1745," *Book Collector*, XII (1963), 21-36, 159-177, 294-307.

Foxon, David. *Libertine Literature in England, 1660-1745*. New Hyde Park, N.Y.: University Books, 1965.

Friedell, Egon. *A Cultural History of the Modern Age*. Volume II. Book two: Baroque and Rococo: from the Thirty Years' War to the Seven Years' War; Book three: Enlightenment and Revolution: from the Seven Years' War to the Congress of Vienna. Translated from the German by Charles Francis Atkinson. New York: Alfred A. Knopf, 1931.

Gay, Peter. *The Enlightenment: An Interpretation. The Rise of Modern Paganism*. Vol. I. New York: Knopf, 1966.

Gay, Peter. "The Enlightenment in the History of Political Theory," *Political Science Quarterly*, LXIX (1954), 374-389.

Gill, Frederick C. *The Romantic Movement and Methodism: A Study of English Romanticism and the Evangelical Revival*. 2nd ed. London: Epworth Press, 1954.

Ginsberg, M. *The Idea of Progress: A Revaluation*. London: Methuen, 1953.

Gloag, John. *Georgian Grace: A Social History of Design from 1600-1830*. New York: Macmillan; London: Black, 1956.

Greenlaw, Edwin. "The New Science and English Literature in the Seventeenth Century," Johns Hopkins Alumni Magazine, XIII (1925), 331-359.

Grierson, H.J.C. The Background of English Literature and Other Collected Essays and Addresses. London: Chatto and Windus, 1925.

Grierson, H.J.C. "Criticism and Creation: Their Interactions," Essays and Studies by Members of the English Association, collected by Una Ellis-Fermor, XXIX (1943; Oxford: Clarendon Press, 1944), 7-29.

Grierson, H.J.C. Cross Currents in English Literature of the XVIIth Century; or the World, the Flesh & the Spirit, their Actions and Reactions. London: Chatto & Windus, 1929.

Guerlac, Henry. "Where the Statue Stood: Divergent Loyalties to Newton in the Eighteenth Century." Aspects of the Eighteenth Century, ed. Earl R. Wasserman (Baltimore: The Johns Hopkins Press, 1965), pp. 317-334.

Hazard, Paul. European Thought in the Eighteenth Century: From Montesquieu to Lessing. Translated by J. Lewis May. London: Hollis & Carter; New Haven, Yale University Press, 1954.

Hazard, Paul. La Crise de la Conscience Européenne (1680-1715). 3 vols. Paris: Boivin, 1934.

Hazard, Paul. La Pensée Européenne au XVIIIe Siècle: de Montesquieu à Lessing. 3 vols. Paris: Boivin, 1946.

Hazard, Paul. The European Mind: The Critical Years, 1680-1715. Trans. J. Lewis May. New Haven and London: Yale Univ. Press, 1953.

Highet, Gilbert. The Classical Tradition: Greek and Roman Influence on Western Literature. New York: Oxford University Press, 1949.

Hill, Christopher. The Century of Revolution, 1603-1714. (A History of England. General Editors: Christopher Brook, and Denis Mark Smith, Vol. V.) Edinburgh: Nelson, 1961.

Houghton, Walter E., Jr. "The English Virtuoso in the Seventeenth Century," JHI, III (1942), 51-73, 190-219.

Humphreys, A.R. *The Augustan World: Life and Letters in Eighteenth-Century England*. London: Methuen, 1954.

Humphreys, A.R. "A Classical Education and Eighteenth-Century Poetry," *Scrutiny*, VIII (1939), 193-207.

Humphreys, A.R. "The Eternal Fitness of Things: An Aspect of Eighteenth Century Thought," *MLR*, XLII (1947), 188-198.

Humphreys, A.R. "'The Friend of Mankind' (1700-60) -- An Aspect of Eighteenth-Century Sensibility," *RES*, XXIV (1948), 203-218.

Humphreys, A.R. "Literature and Religion in Eighteenth-Century England," *Journal of Ecclesiastical History*, III (1952), 159-190.

Hunter, William B., Jr. "The Seventeenth Century Doctrine of Plastic Nature," *Harvard Theological Review*, XLIII (1950), 197-213.

Jeffares, Alexander Norman. *Language, Literature, and Science: An Inaugural Lecture*. Leeds: Leeds University Press, 1959.

Johnson, James W. "Chronological Writing: Its Concepts and Development," *History and Theory*, II (1962), 124-145.

Johnson, James W. "Of Differing Ages and Climes," *JHI*, XXI (1960), 465-468.

Johnson, James W. "That Neo-Classical Bee," *JHI*, XXII (1961), 262-266.

Johnson, James W. "The Scythian: His Rise and Fall," *JHI*, XX (1959), 250-257.

Jones, Richard Foster. *Ancients and Moderns: A Study of the Rise of the Scientific Movement in Seventeenth-Century England*. 2nd ed. Washington University Studies. St. Louis: Washington University, 1961.

Jones, Richard Foster. "The Background of the Attack on Science in the Age of Pope." *Pope and his Contemporaries: Essays Presented to George Sherburn*, ed. James L. Clifford and Louis A. Landa (Oxford: Clarendon Press, 1949), pp. 96-113.

Kennedy, William L. *The English Heritage of Coleridge of Bristol, 1798: The Basis in Eighteenth-Century English Thought for his Distinction between Imagination and Fancy.* (Yale Studies in English, No. 104) New Haven: Yale University Press, 1947.

Kliger, Samuel. "The 'Goths' in England: An Introduction to the Gothic Vogue in Eighteenth-Century Aesthetic Discussion," MP, XLIII (1945), 107-117.

Kliger, Samuel. *The Goths in England: A Study in Seventeenth and Eighteenth Century Thought.* Cambridge, Mass.: Harvard University Press, 1952.

Kliger, Samuel. "Whig Aesthetics: A Phase of Eighteenth Century Taste," ELH, XVI (1949), 135-150.

Knox, Ronald A. *Enthusiasm: A Chapter in the History of Religion, With Special Reference to the Seventeenth and Eighteenth Centuries.* Oxford: Clarendon Press; London: Cumberledge, 1950.

Korniger, Siegfried. *The Restoration Period and the Eighteenth Century, 1660-1780.* Vienna, 1964.

Kramnick, Isaac. "An Augustan Reply to Locke: Bolingbroke on Natural Law and the Origin of Government." *Political Science Quarterly,* LXXXII, (1967), 571-594.

Kramnick, Isaac. *Bolingbroke and His Circle: The Politics of Nostalgia in the Age of Walpole.* Cambridge, Mass.: Harvard University Press, 1968.

Kuhn, Albert J. "English Deism and the Development of Romantic Mythological Syncretism," PMLA, LXII (1956), 1094-1116.

Lamprecht, Sterling P. "Innate Ideas in the Cambridge Platonists," *Philosophical Review,* XXXV (1926), 553-573.

Langer, Suzanne K. *Feeling and Form: A Theory of Art Developed from "Philosophy in a New Key."* New York: Scribner, 1953.

Locke, Louis G. *Tillotson: A Study in Seventeenth-Century Literature.* (Anglistica, Vol. IV.) Copenhagen: Rosenkilde and Bagger, 1954.

Lovejoy, Arthur O. The Great Chain of Being: A Study of the History of an Idea. (The William James Lectures delivered at Harvard University, 1933.) Cambridge, Mass.: Harvard University Press, 1936.

Macdonald, Alastair. "Enthusiasm Resurgent," Dalhousie Review, XVII (1962), 352-363.

Manuel, Frank E. The Eighteenth Century Confronts the Gods. Cambridge, Mass.: Harvard University Press, 1959.

Marlowe, John. The Puritan Tradition in English Life. London: Cresset Press, 1956.

Marshall, John S. "Freedom and Authority in Classical Anglicanism," Anglican Theological Review, XLV (1963), 54-73.

Mazzeo, Joseph Anthony. Renaissance and Revolution: The Remaking of European Thought. New York: Pantheon Books, 1965.

McCloy, Shelby T. "Rationalists and Religion in the Eighteenth Century," South Atlantic Quarterly, XLVI (1947), 467-482.

Milliken, Ernest K. The First Three Georges (1714-1820). London: Harrap, 1958.

Mintz, Samuel I. The Hunting of Leviathan: Seventeenth Century Reactions to the Materialism and Moral Philosophy of Thomas Hobbes. Cambridge: Cambridge University Press, 1962.

Mitchell, W. Fraser. English Pulpit Oratory from Andrewes to Tillotson: A Study of its Literary Aspects. London: S.P.C.K., 1932.

Moore, Cecil A. Backgrounds of English Literature 1700-1760. Minneapolis: University of Minnesota Press, 1953.

Morley, Edith J. "Eighteenth Century Ideals in Life and in Literature," Essays by Divers Hands. Being the Transactions of the Royal Society of Literature of the United Kingdom, XVI (1937), 117-135.

Mornet, Daniel. Thought in the Eighteenth Century, trans. Lawrence M. Levin. New York: Prentice-Hall, 1929.

Murray, John J. "The Cultural Impact of the Flemish Low Countries on Sixteenth- and Seventeenth-Century England," <u>American Historical Review</u>, LXII (1957), 837-854.

Nicolson, Marjorie. <u>Science and Imagination</u>. Ithaca, N.Y.: Cornell University Press; London: Oxford University Press, 1956.

Nicolson, Sir Harold. <u>The Age of Reason (1700-1789)</u>. London: Constable, 1960.

Nussbaum, Frederick L. <u>The Triumph of Science and Reason, 1660-1685</u>. New York: Harper and Brothers, 1953.

Ogilvie, R.M. <u>Latin & Greek: A History of the Influence of the Classics on English Life from 1600 to 1918</u>. London: Routledge; Hamden, Conn.: Archon Books, 1964.

Perdeck, Albert Adam. <u>Theology in Augustan Literature, Being an Inquiry into the Extent of Orthodox Protestant Thought in the Literature of Pope's Time</u>. Groningen: J.B. Wolters, 1928.

Plumb, J.H. <u>Men and Places</u>. London: Cresset Press, 1963.

Plumb, J.H. "Nobility and Gentry in the Early Eighteenth Century," <u>History Today</u>, V (1955), 805-817.

Quennell, Peter. <u>Caroline of England. An Augustan Portrait</u>. New York: Viking, 1940.

Quinlan, Maurice James. <u>Victorian Prelude: A History of English Manners, 1700-1830</u>. (Columbia University Studies in English and Comparative Literature, No. 155.) New York: Columbia University Press, 1941.

Randall, John Herman, Jr. <u>The Career of Philosophy: From the Middle Ages to the Enlightenment</u>. New York: Columbia University Press, 1962.

Raven, Charles E. <u>Natural Religion and Christian Theology</u>. (The Gifford Lectures, 1952. Second Series: Experience and Interpretation.) Cambridge: Cambridge University Press, 1953.

Read, Stanley E. <u>Documents of Eighteenth Century English Taste</u>. Chicago: DePaul Univ. Bookstore, 1942.

Rhys, Hedly Howell (ed.). <u>Seventeenth-Century Science and the Arts</u>. Princeton: Princeton University Press, 1961.

Richardson, A.E. <u>Georgian England. A Survey of Social Life, Trades, Industries and Art from 1700-1820</u>. London: Batsford; New York: Scribner's, 1931.

Sampson, Gregory. <u>The Century of Divine Songs</u>. (Warton Lecture on English Poetry, British Academy, 1943. From the <u>Proceedings of the British Academy</u>, Vol. XXIX.) London: Humphrey Milford, 1943.

Sampson, Ronald Victor. <u>Progress in the Age of Reason: The Seventeenth Century to the Present Age</u>. London: Heinemann; Cambridge, Mass.: Harvard University Press, 1956.

Sams, Henry W. "Anti-stoicism in Seventeenth- and Early Eighteenth-Century England," <u>SP</u>, XLI (1944), 65-78.

Saunders, Beatrice. <u>The Age of Candlelight: The English Social Scene in the Seventeenth Century</u>. London: Centaur Press, 1959.

Schick, George Baldwin. "Appreciation of Milton as a Criterion of Eighteenth-Century Taste," <u>N&Q</u>, CCII (1957), 113-114.

Secord, Arthur W. "Our Indispensable Eighteenth Century," <u>JEGP</u>, XLV (1946), 153-163.

Sells, A. Lytton. <u>The Paradise of Travellers: The Italian Influence on Englishmen in the Seventeenth Century</u>. Indiana University Press, 1964.

Shomberg, Roland N. <u>Religious Liberalism in Eighteenth-Century England</u>. London: Oxford University Press, 1954.

Shorey, Paul. <u>Platonism Ancient and Modern</u>. (Sather Classical Lectures, Vol. XIV) Berkeley: University of California Press, 1938.

Sigworth, Oliver F. "The Four Styles of a Decade (1740-1750)," <u>Bulletin of the New York Public Library</u> LXIV (1960), 407-431.

Smith, Andrew Cannon, S.J. <u>Theories of Nature and Standards of Taste in England, 1700-1790</u>. Chicago (Univ. of Chicago diss., Chap. IV planographed.), 1937.

Smith, Preserved. <u>A History of Modern Culture. Volume I, The Great Renewal, 1543-1687</u>. New York: Henry Holt; London: Routledge, 1930.

Smith, Preserved. A History of Modern Culture. Vol. II. The Enlightenment, 1687-1776. London: Routledge; New York: Henry Holt, 1934.

Spector, Robert. "Late Neo-Classical Taste," N&Q, CXCVI (1951), 11-12.

Steegman, John. The Rule of Taste: From George I to George IV. London: Macmillan, 1936.

Stephen, Sir Leslie. History of English Thought in the Eighteenth Century. 2 vols. London: Murray; New York: Putnam's, 1927.

Stevick, Philip. "The Augustan Nose," UTQ, XXXIV (1965), 110-117.

Stromberg, Roland N. Religious Liberalism in Eighteenth Century England. London: Oxford University Press, 1954.

Suckling, Norman. "The Enlightenment and the Idea of Progress," Studies on Voltaire and the Eighteenth Century, LVIII (1957), 1461-1480.

Sykes, Norman. The English Religious Tradition: Sketches of Its Influence on Church, State, and Society. London: S.C.M. Press, 1953.

Thompson, Elbert N.S. "Mysticism in Seventeenth Century English Literature," SP, XVIII (1921), 170-231.

Turberville, Arthur Stanley. English Men and Manners in the Eighteenth Century: An Illustrated Narrative. Oxford: Clarendon Press, 1926.

Turberville, Arthur Stanley, ed. Johnson's England. An account of the Life and Manners of his Age. 2 vols. Oxford: Clarendon Press, 1933.

Tuveson, Ernest L. Millenium and Utopia: A Study in the Background of the Idea of Progress. Berkeley and Los Angeles: University of California Press, 1949.

Van Leeuwen, Henry G. The Problem of Certainty in English Thought, 1630-1690. With a preface by Richard H. Popkin. (Archives Internationales d'Histoire des Idées / International Archives of the History of Ideas, Vol. 3) The Hague: Nijhoff, 1963.

Walker, Eric A. *The British Empire: Its Structure and Spirit, 1497-1953*. (Studies in Modern European Literature and Thought.) 2nd ed. Cambridge: Bowes and Bowes, 1954.

Ward, Addison. "The Tory View of Roman History," *SEL*, IV (1964), 413-456.

Watt, Ian. "Publishers and Sinners: The Augustan View," *SB*, XII (1959), 3-20.

Wedel, T.O. "On the Philosophical Background of *Gulliver's Travels*," *SP*, XXIII (1926), 434-450.

Westfall, Richard S. *Science and Religion in Seventeenth-Century England*. (Yale Historical Publications, Miscellany No. 67.) New Haven: Yale University Press, 1958.

Whitney, Edward Allen. "Humanitarianism and Romanticism," *HLQ*, II (1939), 159-178.

Whitney, Lois. *Primitivism and the Idea of Progress in English Popular Literature of the Eighteenth Century*. (Contributions to the History of Primitivism.) Baltimore: Johns Hopkins Press; London: Milford, 1934.

Wiley, Margaret L. *The Subtle Knot: Creative Scepticism in Seventeenth-Century England*. Cambridge, Mass: Harvard University Press, 1952.

Willey, Basil. *The Eighteenth Century Background. Studies on the Idea of Nature in the Thought of the Period*. London: Chatto & Windus, 1940.

Willey, Basil. *The Seventeenth-Century Background. Studies in the Thought of the Age in Relation to Poetry and Religion*. London: Chatto and Windus, 1934.

Woodhouse, A.S.P. *The Poet and his Faith: Religion and Poetry in England from Spenser to Eliot and Auden*. Chicago: University of Chicago Press, 1965.

Zagorin, Perez. *A History of Political Thought in the English Revolution*. London: Routledge & Kegan Paul, 1954.

III. Literary History and Criticism:
Literary Theory, Aesthetics, and Stylistics

Abercrombie, Nigel. "Cartesianism and Classicism," MLR, XXXI (1936), 358-376.

Abrams, M.H. "Archetypal Analogies in the Language of Criticism," University of Toronto Quarterly, XVIII (1949), 313-327.

Abrams, Meyer H. The Mirror and the Lamp: Romatic Theory and the Critical Tradition. New York: Oxford University Press, 1953.

Addison, Agnes. Romanticism and the Gothic Revival. New York: Richard R. Smith, 1938.

Aesthetics and Language. Essays, ed. William Elton. New York: Philosophical Library, 1954.

Atkins, J.W.H. English Literary Criticism: Seventeenth and Eighteenth Centuries. London: Methuen, 1951.

Aubin, Robert Arnold. "Some Augustan Gothicists," Harvard Studies and Notes in Philology and Literature, XVII (1935), 15-26.

Auerbach, Erich. Mimesis: The Representation of Reality in Western Literature. Translated from the German by Willard R. Trask. Princeton: Princeton University Press, 1953.

Babcock, Robert W. "English Interest in Italy and Italian Romantic Criticism in the Eighteenth Century," PQ, XXVI (1947), 152-158.

Babcock, Robert W. The Genesis of Shakespeare Idolatry, 1766-1799: A Study in English Criticism of the Late Eighteenth Century. Chapel Hill: University of North Carolina Press, 1931.

Babcock, Robert W. "The Idea of Taste in the Eighteenth Century," PMLA, L (1935), 922-926.

Babcock, Robert W. "A Note on Genius, Imagination and Enthusiasm in Some Late Eighteenth Century Periodicals," N&Q, CXCII (1947), 93-95.

Barker, Arthur. "'...And on his crest sat horror': Eighteenth-Century Interpretations of Milton's Sublimity and his Satan," University of Toronto Quarterly, XI (1942), 421-436.

Baron, Hans. "The *Querelle* of the Ancients and the Moderns as a Problem for Renaissance Scholarship," JHI, XX (1959), 3-22.

Bate, Walter Jackson. *From Classic to Romantic. Premises of Taste in Eighteenth-Century England*. Cambridge, Mass.: Harvard University Press; London: Cumberlege, 1946.

Bate, Walter Jackson. "The Sympathetic Imagination in Eighteenth Century English Criticism," ELH, XII (1945), 144-164.

Bergum, Edwin B. "The Neo-Classical Period in English Literature: A Psychological Definition," Sewanee Review, LII (1944), 247-265.

Binni, Walter. *Classicismo e neoclassicismo nella letteratura del Settecento*. (Studi Critici, 7.) Firenze: La Nuova Italia, 1963.

Boas, George. "In Search of the Age of Reason," Aspects of the Eighteenth Century, ed. Earl R. Wasserman (Baltimore, 1965), pp. 1-19.

Bond, Donald F. "'Distrust' of Imagination in English Neo-Classicism," PQ, XIV (1935), 54-69.

Bond, Donald F. "The Neo-Classical Psychology of the Imagination," ELH, IV (1937), 245-264.

Bosker, Aisso. *Literary Criticism in the Age of Johnson*. Groningen: J.B. Wolters, 1930.

Boyd, John D., S.J. *The Function of Mimesis and Its Decline*. Cambridge, Mass.: Harvard University Press, 1968.

Bredvold, Louis I. "The Gloom of the Tory Satirists," Pope and his Contemporaries: Essays Presented to George Sherburn, ed. James L. Clifford and Louis A. Landa (Oxford: Clarendon Press, 1949), pp. 1-19.

Bredvold, Louis I. "The Literature of the Restoration and Eighteenth Century," A History of English Literature, ed. Hardin Craig (New York: Oxford University Press, 1950), pp. 343-459.

Bredvold, Louis I. "The Rise of English Classicism: A Study in Methodology," Comparative Literature, II (1950), 253-268.

Bredvold, Louis I. "The Tendency Toward Platonism in Neo-Classical Aesthetics," ELH, I (1934), 91-120.

Brett, R.L. "The Aesthetic Sense and Taste in the Literary Criticism of the Early Eighteenth Century," RES, XX (1944), 199-213.

Brett, James Antony. The Triple Stream: Four Centuries of English, French, and German Literature, 1531-1930. Cambridge: Bowes and Bowes, 1953; Philadelphia: Dufour Editions, 1954.

Bronson, Bertrand H. "Personification Reconsidered," ELH, XIV (1947), 163-177.

Bronson, Bertrand H. "The Pre-Romantic or Post-Augustan Mode," ELH, XX (1953), 15-28.

Bronson, Bertrand H. "When was Neo-Classicism?" Studies in Criticism and Aesthetics, 1660-1800: Essays in Honor of Samuel Holt Monk, ed. Howard Anderson and John S. Shea (Minneapolis, Univ. of Minnesota Press, 1967), pp. 13-35.

Brown, Wallace Cable. "A Belated Augustan: Bonnell Thornton, Esq.," PQ, XXXIV (1955), 335-348.

Brown, Wallace Cable. "Dramatic Tension in Neoclassic Satire," College English, VI (1945), 263-269.

Bullitt, John and W.J. Bate. "Distinctions between Fancy and Imagination in Eighteenth Century English Criticism," MLN, LX (1945), 8-15.

Burton, Kathleen M.D. Restoration Literature. (University Library English Literature Series, edited by Basil Willey.) London: Hutchinson, 1955.

Buxton, Charles Roden. A Politician Plays Truant: Essays on English Literature. London: Christophers, 1929.

Cazamian, L. "Histoire de la critique littéraire moderne," Etudes Anglaises, X (1957), 226-230.

Cazamian, Louis. A History of English Literature, Vol. II, Modern Times (1660-1914). New York: Macmillan, 1927.

Cazamian, Louis. The Development of English Humor, Parts I & II. Durham, N.C.: Duke University Press, 1952; London: Cambridge University Press, 1953.

Chandler, Zilpha E. *An Analysis of the Stylistic Technique of Addison, Johnson, Hazlitt and Pater*. (Univ. of Iowa Studies, IV, No. 2). Iowa City: University of Iowa, 1928.

Choudhouri, A.D. "'Happy Mediocrity'--An Augustan Virtue," *Indian Journal of English Studies*, III (1963), 169-174.

Christensen, Francis. "John Wilkins and the Royal Society's Reform of Prose Style," *MLQ*, VII (1946), 179-187, 279-90.

Churchill, R.C. *English Literature of the Eighteenth Century. With a Preface on the Relations between Literary History and Literary Criticism*. London: University Tutorial Press, 1953.

Clifford, James L. "The Eighteenth Century," *MLQ*, XXVI (1965), 111-134.

Cochrane, Rexmond C. "Francis Bacon in Early Eighteenth-Century English Literature," *PQ*, XXXVII (1958), 58-79.

Constantine, J. Robert. "The Ignoble Savage, an Eighteenth Century Literary Stereotype," *Phylon*, XXVII (1966), 171-179.

Cope, Jackson I. "Seventeenth-Century Quaker Style," *PMLA*, LXII (1956), 725-754.

Crane, Ronald S. "English Neoclassical Criticism: An Outline Sketch," *Critics and Criticism Ancient and Modern* (Chicago, 1952), pp. 372-388.

Crane, Ronald S. "A Neglected Mid Eighteenth-Century Plea for Originality and Its Author," *PQ* XIII (1934), 21-29.

Crane, Ronald S. "On Writing the History of English Criticism, 1650-1800," *UTQ*, XXII (1953), 376-391.

Crutwell, Patrick. "The Eighteenth Century: A Classical Age?" *Arion*, VII (1967), 110-132.

Daiches, David. *Critical Approaches to Literature*. Englewood Cliffs: Prentice Hall, 1956.

Daiches, David. *A Critical History of English Literature*. 2 vols. London: Secker & Warburg, 1960.

Davie, Donald, "Augustans New and Old," *Twentieth Century*, CLVIII (1955), 464-475.

Davie, Donald. *The Language of Science and the Language of Literature, 1700-1740*. London: Sheed and Ward, 1963.

Davis, Herbert. "The Conversation of the Augustans," *The Seventeenth Century: Studies in the History of English Thought and Literature from Bacon to Pope, by Richard Foster Jones and Others Writing in His Honor* (Stanford: Stanford University Press, 1951), pp. 181-197.

Davis, Herbert. "The Correspondence of the Augustans," *Essays in English Literature from the Renaissance to the Victorian Age Presented to A.S.P. Woodhouse*, ed. Millar Maclure and F.W. Watt (Toronto, Univ. of Toronto Press, 1964), pp. 195-212.

Dieckmann, Herbert. "An Interpretation of the Eighteenth Century," *MLQ*, XV (1954), 295-311.

Dobrée, Bonamy. *English Literature in the Early Eighteenth Century, 1700-1740*. (Oxford History of English Literature, Vol. VII.) Oxford: Clarendon Press, 1959.

Draper, John. "Aristotelian 'Mimesis' in Eighteenth Century England," *PMLA*, XXXVI (1921), 372-400.

Draper, John W. "The Rise of English Neo-Classicism," *Revue Anglo-Américaine*, X (1933), 399-409.

Draper, John W. "The Theory of the Comic in Eighteenth Century England," *JEGP*, XXXVII (1938), 207-223.

Draper, John W. "The Theory of Translation in the Eighteenth Century," *Neophilologus*, VI (1921), 241-254.

Elledge, Scott. "The Background and Development in English Criticism of the Theories of Generality and Particularity," *PMLA*, LXII (1947), 147-182.

Elton, Oliver. *A Survey of English Literature, 1730-1780*. London: Edward Arnold, 1928.

Erskine-Hill, Howard. "Augustans on Augustanism: England, 1655-1759," *RMS*, XI (1967), 55-83.

Fisch, Harold. "The Puritans and the Reform of Prose Style, " *ELH*, XIX (1952), 229-248.

Fisher, Peter F. "Blake's Attack on the Classical Tradition," PQ, XL (1961), 1-18.

Fleischmann, Wolfgang Bernhard. "Classicism," Encyclopedia of Poetry and Poetics, ed. Alex Preminger, Frank J. Warnke, and O.B. Hardison, Jr. (Princeton: Princeton University Press, 1965), pp. 136-141.

Fleischmann, Wolfgang Bernhard. Lucretius and English Literature, 1680-1740. Paris: A.G. Nizet, 1964.

Foerster, Donald M. Homer in English Criticism. The Historical Approach to the Eighteenth Century. (Yale Studies in English, Vol. 105.) New Haven: Yale University Press; London: Cumberlege, 1947.

Ford, Franklin L. "The Enlightenment: Towards a Useful Redefinition," Studies in the Eighteenth Century, ed. R.F. Brissenden (Canberra: Australian National University Press, 1968), pp. 17-29.

Frankel, Paul. The Gothic: Literary Sources and Interpretation through Eight Centuries. Princeton: Princeton University Press, 1960.

Fraser, Ray. "The Origin of the Term 'Image,'" ELH, XXVII (1960), 149-161.

Freimarck, Vincent. "The Bible and Neo-Classical Views of Style," JEGP, LI (1952), 507-526.

Fussell, Paul. The Rhetorical World of Augustan Humanism: Ethics and Imagery from Swift to Burke. Oxford: Clarendon Press, 1965.

Galloway, Francis. Reason, Rule, and Revolt in English Classicism. New York: Scribner's, 1940.

Gardner, Helen. The Limits of Literary Criticism: Reflections on the Interpretations of Poetry and Science. (Riddell Memorial Lectures, No. 28.) London: Oxford University Press, 1956.

Gilbert, Allan H., and Snuggs, Henry L. "On the Relation of Horace to Aristotle in Literary Criticism," JEGP, XLVI (1947), 233-247.

Goldberg, M.A. "Wit and the Imagination in Eighteenth Century Aesthetics," JAAC, XVI (1958), 503-509.

Goodman, Paul. "Neo-classicism, Platonism, and Romanticism," *Journal of Philosophy*, XXXI (1934), 148-163.

Green, F.C. *Minuet: A Critical Survey of French and English Literary Ideas in the Eighteenth Century*. London: Dent; New York: Dutton, 1935.

Greene, Donald J. "Augustinianism and Empiricism: A Note on Eighteenth-Century English Intellectual History," *Eighteenth-Century Studies*, I (1967), 33-68.

Greene, Donald J. "The Sin of Pride: A Sketch for a Literary Exploration," *New Mexico Quarterly*, XXXIV (1964-5), 8-30.

Greene, Donald J. "The Uses of Autobiography in the Eighteenth Century," *Essays in Eighteenth-Century Biography*, ed., with an introduction, by Philip B. Daghlian (Bloomington, Ind., 1968), pp. 43-66.

Greenlaw, Edwin. "Modern English Romanticism," *SP*, XXII (1925), 538-550.

Haller, Elizabeth. *Die Barocken Stilmerkmale in der Englischen, Lateinischen, und Deutschen Fassung von Dr. Thomas Burnets "Theory of the Earth."* (Schweizer Anglistische Arbeiten, Band IX.) Bern: Verlag A. Franke, 1940.

Hamm, Victor M. "The Problem of Form in Nature and the Arts," *JAAC*, XII (1954), 175-184.

Havens, Raymond D. "Changing Taste in the Eighteenth Century, A Study of Dryden's and Dodsley's Miscellanies," *PMLA*, XLIV (1929), 501-536.

Havens, Raymond D. "Simplicity, A Changing Concept," *JHI*, XIV (1953), 3-32.

Havens, Raymond D. "Solitude and the Neo-classicists," *ELH*, XXI (1954), 251-273.

Henn, T.R. *Longinus and English Criticism*. Cambridge: Cambridge University Press, 1934.

Hipple, Walter J., Jr. *The Beautiful, the Sublime, & the Picturesque in Eighteenth Century British Aesthetic Theory*. Carbondale: University of Southern Illinois Press, 1957.

Hipple, Walter J., Jr. "Philosophical Language and the Theory of Beauty in the Eighteenth Century," <u>Studies in Criticism and Aesthetics, 1660-1800: Essays in Honor of Samuel Holt Monk</u>, ed. Howard Anderson and John S. Shea (Minneapolis, 1967), pp. 213-231.

Hooker, Edward Niles. "The Discussion of Taste, from 1750 to 1770, and the New Trends in Literary Criticism," <u>PMLA</u>, XLIX (1934), 577-592.

Hooker, Edward N. "Humour in the Age of Pope," <u>HLQ</u>, XI (1948), 361-385.

Hooker, Edward N. "The Reviewers and the New Criticism, 1754-1770," <u>PQ</u>, XII (1934), 189-202; and <u>MLN</u>, XI (1936), 207-214.

Horace. <u>Horace: Three Phases of his Influence</u>. Lectures given at Mount Holyoke College in celebration of the Bimillenium Horatianum, 1935, by Paul Frederic Saintonge, Leslie Gale Brugevin, and Helen Griffith. Chicago: University of Chicago Press, 1936.

Howell, A.C. "<u>Res et verba</u>: Words and Things," <u>ELH</u>, XIII (1946), 131-142.

Hughes, Richard E. "'Wit': The Genealogy of a Theory," <u>CLA Journal</u>, V (1961), 142-144.

Hyman, Stanley Edgar. <u>Poetry and Criticism: Four Revolutions in Literary Taste</u>. New York: Atheneum, 1961.

Irving, William Henry. <u>The Providence of Wit in the English Letter Writers</u>. Durham, N.C.: Duke University Press, 1955.

Jackson, Wallace. "Affective Values in Early Eighteenth-Century Aesthetics," <u>JAAC</u>, XXXVII (1968), 87-92.

Johnson, James W. <u>The Formation of English Neo-Classical Thought</u>. Princeton: Princeton Univ. Press, 1967.

Johnson, James W. "The Meaning of 'Augustan,'" <u>JHI</u>, XIX (1958), 507-522.

Johnston, Arthur. <u>Enchanted Ground: The Study of Medieval Romance in the Eighteenth Century</u>. London: Athlone Press, 1964.

Jones, Richard Foster. *Ancients and Moderns: A Study of the Background of the Battle of the Books.* Washington University Studies, Language and Literature, No. 6. St. Louis: Washington University Press, 1936.

Jones, Richard Foster. "The Attack on Pulpit Eloquence in the Restoration: An Episode in the Development of the Neoclassical Standard for Prose," *JEGP*, XXX (1931), 188-217.

Jones, Richard Foster. "Science and Criticism in the Neoclassical Age of English Literature," *JHI*, I (1940), 381-412.

Jones, Richard Foster. "Science and English Prose Style in the Third Quarter of the Seventeenth Century," *PMLA*, XLV (1930), 977-1009.

Jones, William Powell. "The Captive Linnet: A Footnote on Eighteenth Century Sentiment," *PQ*, XXXIII (1954), 330-337.

Jones, William Powell. "Science in Biblical Paraphrases in Eighteenth Century England," *PMLA*, LXXIV (1959), 41-51.

Jörgensen, Bodil. "Aesthetic Criticism in England from 1675-1725: Some Problems," *Orbis Litterarum*, II (1944-45), 43-66.

Joshi, K.L. "Augustan Age," *TLS*, 10 July 1937, p. 512.

Kallich, Martin. "The Argument Against the Association of Ideas in Eighteenth Century Aesthetics," *MLQ*, XV (1954), 125-136.

Kallich, Martin. "The Association of Ideas and Critical Theory: Hobbes, Locke and Addison," *ELH*, XII (1945), 290-315.

Kallich, Martin. "The Associationist Criticism of Francis Hutcheson and David Hume," *SP*, XLIII (1946), 644-647.

Knox, Norman. *The Word 'Irony' and its Context, 1500-1755.* Durham: Duke University Press, 1961.

Leedy, Paul F. "Genres Criticism and the Significance of Warton's *Essay on Pope*," *JEGP*, XLV (1946), 140-146.

Leonard, Sterling Andrus. *The Doctrine of Correctness in English Usage, 1700-1800.* Univ. of Wisconsin Stud. in Language and Literature, No. 25. Madison, 1929.

Lewis, Clive Staples. *Studies in Words*. Cambridge: Cambridge University Press, 1960.

Lewis, Saunders. *A School of Welsh Augustans: Being a Study in English Influences on Welsh Literature during Part of the Eighteenth Century*. Wrexham: Hughes; London: Simkin Marshall, 1924.

Lipking, Lawrence. "The Shifting Nature of Authority in Versions of *De Arte Graphica*," *Journal of Aesthetics and Art Criticism*, XXIII (1965), 487-504.

Longueil, Alfred E. "The Word 'Gothic' in Eighteenth Century Criticism," *MLN*, XXXVIII (1923), 453-460.

Lovejoy, Arthur O. "'Nature' as Aesthetic Norm," *MLN*, XLII (1927), 444-450.

Lovejoy, Arthur O. "Optimism and Romanticism," *PMLA*, XLII (1927), 921-945.

Lovejoy, Arthur O. "The Parallel of Deism and Classicism," *MP*, XXIX (1932), 281-299.

Lucas, Frank L. *Style*. London: Cassell, 1955.

Luck, Georg. "Scriptor Classicus," *Comparative Literature*, X (1958), 150-158.

McCutcheon, Roger P. "Eighteenth Century Aesthetics: A Search for Surviving Values," *Harvard Library Bulletin*, X (1956), 287-305.

McCutcheon, Roger P. *Eighteenth-Century English Literature*. (Home University Library.) Oxford: Oxford University Press; London: Cumberlege, 1950.

McDermott, Douglas. "George Campbell and the Classical Tradition," *Quarterly Journal of Speech*, XLIX (1963), 403-409.

MacDonald, W.L. "The Augustan 'Mobility'," *UTQ*, II (1933), 200-216.

MacDonald, W.L. "Augustan Personalities," *Queens Quarterly*, LVI (1949), 221-230.

McKenzie, Gordon. *Critical Responsiveness: A Study of the Psychological Current in Later Eighteenth-Century Criticism.* (University of California Publications in English, Vol. XX.) Berkeley and Los Angeles: University of California Press, 1949.

McKeon, Richard. "Literary Criticism and the Concept of Imitation in Antiquity." *MP*, XXIV (1936), 1-35.

McKeon, Richard. *Thought, Action and Passion.* Chicago: University of Chicago Press, 1954.

McKillop, Alan Dugald. *English Literature from Dryden to Byron.* New York: Appleton-Century-Crofts, 1948.

Mann, Elizabeth L. "The Problem of Originality in English Literary Criticism 1750-1800," *PQ*, XVIII (1939), 97-118.

Marks, Emerson R. *The Poetics of Reason. English Neoclassical Criticism.* (Studies in Language and Literature, 22). New York: Random House, 1968.

Marks, Emerson R. *Relativist and Absolutist: The Early Neo-Classical Debate in England.* New Brunswick, N.J.: Rutgers University Press, 1955.

Maurer, Wallace. "From Renaissance to Neo-Classic," *N&Q*, CCIII (1958), 287.

Maurocordato, Alexandre. *La Critique classique en Angleterre de la Restauration à la mort de Joseph Addison: Essai de définition.* Paris: Didier, 1964.

Maxwell, J.C. "'Classic,'" *N&Q*, CCVIII (1963), 220.

Maxwell, J.C. "Demigods & Pickpockets: The Augustan Myth in Swift and Rousseau," *Scrutiny*, XI (1942), 34-39.

Milburn, Daniel Judson. *The Age of Wit, 1650-1750.* New York: Macmillan, 1966.

Monk, Samuel Holt. "'A Grace Beyond the Reach of Art'," *JHI*, V (1944), 131-150.

Monk, Samuel Holt. "From Jacobean to Augustan," *Southern Review*, VII (1941), 366-384.

Monk, Samuel Holt. *The Sublime: A Study of Critical Theories in XVIII-Century England*. New York: Modern Language Association of America, 1935.

Moore, John Robert. "Milton among the Augustans: The Infernal Council," *SP*, XLVIII (1951), 15-25.

Mueller, William R. *Spenser's Critics: Changing Currents in Literary Taste*. Syracuse: Syracuse University Press, 1959.

Murray, John Middleton. *Discoveries: Essays in Literary Criticism*. London: Collins, 1924.

Nahm, Milton C. "The Relation of Aesthetics and Criticism," *Personalist*, XLV (1964), 362-384.

Nicolson, Marjorie Hope. *Mountain Gloom and Mountain Glory: The Development of the Aesthetics of the Infinite*. Ithaca, N.Y.: Cornell University Press, 1959.

Nicolson, Marjorie Hope. "The 'new astronomy' and English literary imagination," *SP*, XXXII (1935), 428-462.

Oakes, Frances E. "Neo-classic Literary Theory as an Outgrowth of the Eighteenth-Century Climate of Opinion," *Florida State University Studies*, VI (1952), 11-22.

Ogden, Henry V.S. "The Principles of Variety and Contrast in Seventeenth Century Aesthetics, and Milton's Poetry," *JHI*, X (1949), 159-182.

Ogden, Henry V.S. "Thomas Burnet's *Telluris Theoria Sacra* and Mountain Scenery," *ELH*, XIV (1947), 139-150.

Osborne, Harold. *Aesthetics and Criticism*. London: Routledge & Kegan Paul, 1955.

Parnell, Paul E. "The Sentimental Mask," *PMLA*, LXXVIII (1963), 529-535.

Partridge, Eric. "The 1762 efflorescence of Poetics," *SP*, XXV (1928), 27-35.

Pettit, Henry. "The Limits of Reason as Literary Theme in the English Enlightenment," Transactions of the First International Congress on the Enlightenment (Studies on Voltaire and the Eighteenth Century, Vols. XXIV, XXV, XXVI, and XXVII), ed. Theodore Besterman (Geneva: Institut et Musée Voltaire, 1963), pp. 1307-1319.

Pettit, Henry. "The Pleasing Paths of Sense: The Subject-Matter of Augustan Literature," Literature and Science (International Federation for Modern Languages and Literatures: Proceedings of the Sixth Terminal Congress, Oxford, 1954.) (Oxford: Blackwell, 1955), pp. 169-174.

Popkin, Richard H. "Skepticism in the Enlightenment," Transactions of the First International Congress on the Enlightenment (Studies on Voltaire and the Eighteenth Century, Vols.XXIV, XXV, XXVI, and XXVII), ed. Theodore Besterman (Geneva: Institut et Musée Voltaire, 1963), pp. 1321-1345.

Praz, Mario. Gusto Neoclassico. Florence, 1940. Published in English as: On Neoclassicism, trans. from the Italian by Angus Davidson. London: Thames & Hudson, 1969.

Price, John V. "Concepts of Enlightenment in Eighteenth-Century Scottish Literature," TSLL, IX (1967), 371-379.

Price, Martin. To the Palace of Wisdom: Studies in Order and Energy from Dryden to Blake. Garden City, N.Y.: Doubleday, 1964.

Purpus, Eugene R. "The 'plain, easy, and familiar way': the Dialogue in English Literature, 1660-1725," ELH, XVII (1950), 47-58.

Ramondt, Marie. "Between Laughter and Humour in the Eighteenth Century," Neophilologus, XL (1956), 128-138.

Ramsey, Paul. The Lovely and the Just: An Argument for Propriety. (University of Alabama Studies, 15.) Birmingham, Ala.: University of Alabama Press, 1962.

Rapp, Albert. The Origins of Wit and Humor. New York, 1951.

Robertson, J.G. The Reconciliation of Classic and Romantic. ("Publications of the Modern Humanities Research Association," No. 8). Cambridge: Bowes and Bowes, 1925.

Rodway, Allan. "By Algebra to Augustanism," English Studies Presented to R.W. Zandvoort (Amsterdam, 1964), pp. 53-67.

Røstvig, Maren-Sofie. The Background of English Neo-Classicism: With Some Comments on Swift and Pope. Oslo: Universitetsforl, 1961.

Røstvig, Maren-Sofie. The Happy Man: Studies in the Metamorphoses of a Classical Ideal. Vol. I, 1600-1700. Vol. II, 1700-1760. 2 vols. Oslo and Oxford, 1954-58. 2nd ed. of Vol. I (Oslo Studies in English, No. 2); Oslo: Norwegian Universities Press, 1962.

Saintsbury, George. A History of English Criticism: Being the English Chapters of "A History of Criticism and Literary Taste in Europe." Revised, Adapted, and Supplemented. London: Blackwood, 1922.

Saintsbury, George. The Peace of the Augustans: A Survey of Eighteenth Century Literature as a Place of Rest and Refreshment. With an introduction by Sir Herbert Grierson. (World's Classics.) Oxford: Oxford University Press, 1946.

Scheffer, John D. "The idea of decline in literature and the fine arts in eighteenth-century England," MP, XXIV (1936), 155-178.

Schilling, Bernard N. (ed.) Essential Articles For the Study of English Augustan Backgrounds. Hamden, Conn.: Archon Books, 1961.

Sesmat, Augustin. Le système absolu classique et les mouvements réels. Etude historique et critique. Paris, Hermann, 1936.

Sewell, Arthur. "The Concept of Character in the Eighteenth Century," Litera, IV (1957), 2-21.

Shackleton, Robert. "Comparative Literature and the Enlightenment," Comparative Literature: Proceedings of the Second Congress of the International Comparative Literature Association, ed. Werner P. Friedrich (Chapel Hill: Univ. of North Carolina Press, 1959), pp. 56-61.

Sherburn, George. "The Restoration and Eighteenth Century (1660-1789)," A Literary History of England, ed. Albert C. Baugh (New York and London: Appleton-Century-Crofts, 1948), pp. 697-1108.

Simon, Irène. "Critical Terms in Restoration Translations from the French," <u>Revue Belge de Philologie et d'Histoire</u>, XLII (1964), 843-879.

Simon, Irène. "'Pride of Reason' in the Restoration," <u>Revue des Langues Vivantes</u>, XXV (1949), 375-396, 453-473.

Singer, Irving. "The Language of Aesthetics," <u>Hudson Review</u>, IX (1956), 226-243.

Smith, David Nicol. <u>Shakespeare in the Eighteenth Century</u>. Oxford: Clarendon Press, 1928.

Smith, Harold Wendell. "'Reason' and the Restoration Ethos," <u>Scrutiny</u>, XVIII (1951), 118-36.

Spencer, Terence. <u>Fair Greece Sad Relic: Literary Philhellenism from Shakespeare to Byron</u>. London: Weidenfeld and Nicolson, 1954.

Stephens, John C. Jr. "'Classic' and 'Romantic'," <u>Emory University Quarterly</u>, XV (1959), 212-219.

Stern, Bernard Herbert. <u>The Rise of Romantic Hellenism in English Literature, 1732-1786</u>. Menasha, Wis.: Banta, 1940.

Stolnitz, Jerome. "On the Origins of 'Aesthetic Disinterestedness,'" <u>JAAC</u>, XX (1961), 131-143.

Stone, George Winchester, Jr. "Shakespeare in the Periodicals, 1700-1740: A Study of the Growth of a Knowledge of the Dramatist in the Eighteenth Century (Part II)," <u>Shakespeare Quarterly</u>, III (1952), 313-328.

Suckling, Norman. "A Further Contribution to the Classic-Romantic Debate," <u>Durham University Journal</u>, XXXIX (1946), 20-26.

Swedenberg, H.T., Jr. "Fable, Action, Unity and Supernatural Machinery in English Epic Theory, 1650-1800," <u>ES</u>, LXXIII (1938), 39-48.

Swedenberg, H.T., Jr. "Rules and English Critics of the Epic, 1650-1800," <u>SP</u>, XXIV (1938), 54-62.

Swedenberg, H.T., Jr. <u>The Theory of the Epic in England, 1650-1800</u>. (University of California Publications in English, Vol. XV.) Berkeley and Los Angeles: University of California Press, 1944.

Tave, Stuart M. *The Amiable Humorist: A Study in the Comic Theory and Criticism of the Eighteenth and Early Nineteenth Centuries.* Chicago: University of Chicago Press, 1960.

Taylor, Houghton W. "'Particular Character': An Early Phase of a Literary Evolution," *PMLA*, LX (1945), 479-494.

Thomas, P.G. *Aspects of Literary Theory and Practice, 1550-1870.* London: Heath Cranton, 1931.

Thomson, James A.K. *The Classical Background of English Literature.* London: Allen and Unwin; New York: Macmillan, 1948.

Thomson, James A.K. *Classical Influence on English Prose.* London: Alten & Unwin, 1956.

Thorpe, Clarence D. "Two Augustans Cross the Alps: Dennis and Addison on Mountain Scenery," *SP*, XXXII (1935), 463-482.

Tillotson, Geoffrey. *Augustan Studies.* London: Athlone Press; New York: Oxford University Press, 1961.

Tillotson, Geoffrey. *Essays in Criticism and Research.* Cambridge: At the University Press; New York: Macmillan Co., 1942.

Tucker, Susie I. *Protean Shape, A Study in Eighteenth-Century Vocabulary and Usage.* University of London: The Athlone Press, 1967.

Tuveson, Ernest Lee. *The Imagination as a Means of Grace: Locke and the Aesthetics of Romanticism.* Berkeley and Los Angeles: University of California Press, 1960.

Tuveson, Ernest L. "Space, Deity, and the 'Natural Sublime,'" *MLQ*, XII (1951), 20-38.

Ustick, W. Lee, and Hudson, Hoyt H. "Wit, 'mixt wit', and the Bee in Amber," *Huntington Library Bulletin,* No. 8, October 1935, pp. 103-130.

Vines, Sherard. *The Course of English Classicism.* London: Hogarth Press; New York: Harcourt, Brace and Co., 1930.

Voitle, Robert. "The Reason of the English Enlightenment," <u>Transactions of the First International Congress on the Enlightenment</u> (Studies on Voltaire and the Eighteenth Century, Vols, XXIV, XXV, XXVI, and XXVII), ed. Theodore Besterman (Geneva: Institut et Musée Voltaire, 1963), pp. 1735-1774.

Von Erhardt-Siebold, Erika. "Some Inventions of the Pre-Romantic Period and their Influence Upon Literature," <u>ES</u>, LXVI (1932), 347-363.

Wadsworth, Philip A. "A Formula of Literary Criticism, from Aristotle to La Bruyère," <u>MLQ</u>, VII (1946), 35-42.

Walton, Geoffrey. <u>Metaphysical to Augustan: Studies in Tone and Sensibility in the Seventeenth Century</u>. London: Bowes & Bowes, 1955.

Wasserman, Earl R. "Another Eighteenth Century Distinction between Fancy and Imagination," <u>MLN</u>, LXIV (1949), 23-25.

Wasserman, Earl R. "The Inherent Values of Eighteenth-Century Personification," <u>PMLA</u>, LXV (1950), 435-463.

Wasserman, Earl R. "Nature Moralized: The Divine Analogy in the Eighteenth Century," <u>ELH</u>, XX (1953), 39-76.

Wasserman, Earl R. "The scholarly origin of the Elizabethan Revival," <u>ELH</u>, IV (1937), 213-243.

Watson, George. "Contributions to a Dictionary of Critical Terms: Imagination and Fancy," <u>EC</u>, III (1953), 201-214.

Watson, George. <u>The Literary Critics: A Study of English Descriptive Criticism</u>. Harmondsworth and Baltimore: Penguin Books, 1962.

Watt, Ian, ed. <u>The Augustan Age: Approaches to Its Literature, Life, and Thought</u>. Greenwich, Conn.; 1968.

Watt, Ian. "Three Aspects of the Augustan Tradition," <u>Listener</u>, LXXVII (1967), 454, 456-457; 489-491; 553-555.

Watt, Ian. "Two Historical Aspects of the Augustan Tradition," <u>Studies in the Eighteenth Century</u>, ed. R.F. Brissenden (Canberra: Australian National University Press, 1968), pp. 67-88.

Wedgwood, C.V. *Seventeenth-century English Literature*. (Home University Library.) Oxford University Press; London: Cumberlege, 1950.

Weinbrot, Howard D. "Parody as Imitation in the Eighteenth Century," *A N & Q*, II (1964), 131-134.

Weinbrot, Howard D. "The Pattern of Formal Verse Satire in the Restoration and Eighteenth Century," *PMLA*, LXXX (1965), 394-401.

Weinbrot, Howard D. "Translation and Parody: Towards the Genealogy of the Augustan Imitation," *ELH*, XXXIII (1966), 434-447.

Weisbach, Werner. "Die Klassische Ideologie: Ihre Entstehung und Ihre Ausbreitung in den Kuenstlerischen Vorstellung der Neuzeit," *Deutsche Vierteljahrschrift fuer Literaturwissenschaft und Geistesgeschichte*, XI (1933), 559-591.

Wellek, René. "The Concept of Baroque in Literary Scholarship," *JAAC*, V (1946), 77-109.

Wellek, René. "The Concept of Evolution in Literary History," *For Roman Jakobson: Essays on the Occasion of his Sixtieth Birthday*, ed. Morris Halle and others (The Hague: Mouton & Co., 1956), pp. 653-661.

Wellek, René. "The Concept of 'Romanticism' in Literary History: I. The Term 'Romantic' and its Derivatives; II. The Unity of European Romanticism," *Comparative Literature*, I (1949), 1-23, 147-172.

Wellek, René. *A History of Modern Criticism, 1750-1950*. Vol. I: *The Later Eighteenth Century*. Yale University Press, 1955.

Wellek, René. *The Rise of English Literary History*. Chapel Hill: Univ. of North Carolina Press, 1941.

Wellek, René. "The Term and Concept of 'Classicism' in Literary History," *Aspects of the Eighteenth Century*, ed. Earl R. Wasserman (Baltimore, 1965), pp. 105-128.

Wells, Henry W. *New Poets from Old. A Study in Literary Genetics*. New York: Columbia University Press, 1940.

West, Albert H. *L'Influence Française dans la Poesie Burlesque en Angleterre Entre 1660 et 1700*. Paris: Champion, 1930.

Wild, Friedrich. "Zum Problem des Barocks in der Englischen Dichtung," *Anglia*, LIX (1935), 414-422.

Williamson, George. "The Restoration Revolt Against Enthusiasm," *SP* XXX (1933), 571-603.

Williamson, George. "The Rhetorical Pattern of Neoclassical Wit," *MP*, XXXIII (1935), 55-81.

Williamson, George. *The Senecan Amble: A Study in Prose Form from Bacon to Collier*. London: Faber and Faber; Chicago: University of Chicago Press, 1951.

Williamson, George. "Senecan Style in the Seventeenth Century," *PQ*, XV (1936), 321-351.

Wilson, Mona. "The Twilight of the Augustans," *Essays and Studies by Members of the English Association*, XX (1935), 75-85.

Wimsatt, W.K., Jr. *Hateful Contraries: Studies in Literature and Criticism*. Lexington, Ky.: University of Kentucky Press, 1965.

Wimsatt, W.K., Jr., and Cleanth Brooks. *Literary Criticism: A Short History*. New York: Knopf, 1957.

Wimsatt, W.K., Jr. "The Structure of the 'Concrete Universal' in Literature," *PMLA*, LXII (1947), 262-280.

Wood, Paul Spencer. "Native Elements in English Neo-Classicism," *MP*, XXIV (1926), 201-208.

Wood, Paul Spencer. "The Opposition to Neo-classicism in England between 1660 and 1700," *PMLA*, XLIII (1928), 182-197.

Wright, Herbert G. "The Theme of Solitude and Retirement in Seventeenth Century Literature." *Etudes Anglaises*, VII (1954), 22-35.

Youngren, William. "Generality in Augustan Satire," *In Defense of Reading*, ed. R.A. Brower and R. Poirier. (New York, 1962), pp. 206-234.

Ziff, Larzer. "The Literary Consequences of Puritanism." *ELH*, XXX (1963), 293-305.

IV.  Poetics

Alvarez, Alfred.  The School of Donne.  London:  Chatto and Windus, 1961.

Arthos, John.  "Poetic Diction and Scientific Language," Isis, XXXII, (1949 for 1940), 324-338.

Arthos, John.  The Language of Natural Description in Eighteenth-Century Poetry.  (University of Michigan Publications:  Language and Literature Series, xxiv.)  Ann Arbor:  University of Michigan Press, 1949.

Aubin, Robert Arnold.  Topographical Poetry in Eighteenth-Century England.  New York:  The Modern Language Association of America; London:  Milford, 1936.

Bate, Walter Jackson.  "The English Poet and the Burden of the Past, 1660-1820," Aspects of the Eighteenth Century, ed. Earl R. Wasserman (Baltimore, 1965), pp. 245-264.

Bevan, Alan.  "Poetry and Politics in Restoration England," Dalhousie Review, XXXIX (1959), 314-325.

Bond, Richmond P.  English Burlesque Poetry, 1700-1750.  (Harvard Studies in English, vi.)  Cambridge, Mass.:  Harvard University Press, 1932.

Bradner, Leicester.  Musae Anglicanae.  A History of Anglo-Latin Poetry, 1500-1925.  (Modern Language Association of America, General Series, X.)  New York:  Modern Language Association of America, 1940.

Bragg, Marion K.  The Formal Eclogue in Eighteenth-Century England. University of Maine Studies, Second series, No. 6.  Orono, Maine, 1926.

Brooks, Harold F.  "The 'Imitation' in English Poetry, Especially in Formal Satire, Before the Age of Pope," RES, XXV (1949), 124-140.

Brower, Reuben A.  "Form and Defect of Form in Eighteenth-Century Poetry: A Memorandum," CE, XXIX (1968), 535-541.

Brown, Wallace Cable.  The Triumph of Form:  A Study of the Later Masters of the Heroic Couplet.  Chapel Hill, N.C.:  University of North Carolina Press, 1948.

Bush, Douglas. *English Poetry: The Main Currents from Chaucer to the Present*. New York: Oxford University Press, 1952.

Butt, John. "Science and Man in Eighteenth-Century Poetry," *Durham University Journal*, XXXIX (n.s. VIII) (1947), 79-88.

Chapin, Chester F. *Personification in Eighteenth-Century English Poetry*. New York: King's Crown Press, 1955.

Chernaik, Warren A. "The Heroic Occasional Poem: Panegyric and Satire in the Restoration," *MLQ*, XXVI (1965), 523-535.

Cohen, Ralph. "Association of Ideas and Poetic Unity," *PQ*, XXXVI (1957), 465-474.

Cohen, Ralph. "The Augustan Mode in English Poetry," *Eighteenth-Century Studies*, I (1967), 3-32.

Collins, H.P. "A Note on the Classical Principle in Poetry," *Criterion*, III (1925), 389-400.

Congleton, James E. "The Effect of the Restoration on Poetry," *Tennessee Studies in Literature*, VI (1961), 43-101.

Congleton, James E. "Theories of Pastoral Poetry in England, 1684-1717," *SP*, XLI (1944), 544-575.

Congleton, James E. *Theories of Pastoral Poetry in England, 1684-1798*. Gainesville: University of Florida Press, 1952.

Cook, Albert S. *The Classic Line: A Study in Epic Poetry*. Bloomington: Indiana University Press, 1966.

Cooper, Lane. *The Poetics of Aristotle: Its Meaning and Influence*. Ithaca, New York: Cornell University Press, 1956.

Crane, Ronald S. *The Languages of Criticism and the Structure of Poetry*. (The Alexander Lectures, 1951-52.) Toronto: University of Toronto Press, 1953.

Davie, Donald. *Purity of Diction in English Verse*. London: Chatto & Windus, 1952; New York: Oxford University Press, 1953.

Deane, Cecil V. *Aspects of Eighteenth Century Nature Poetry*. Oxford: Blackwell, 1935.

Dobrée, Bonamy. "Milton and Dryden: A Comparison and Contrast in Poetic Ideas and Poetic Method," ELH, III (1936), 83-100.

Dobrée, Bonamy. "Nature Poetry in the Early Eighteenth Century," E&S, XVIII (1965), 13-33.

Dobrée, Bonamy. "The Theme of Patriotism in the Poetry of the Early Eighteenth Century," Proceedings of the British Academy, XXXV (1949), 49-65.

Doubleday, N.F. Studies in Poetry. New York, 1949.

Draper, John W. The Funeral Elegy and the Rise of English Romanticism. New York: New York University Press, 1929.

Draper, John W. "The Metrical Tale in XVIII-century England," PMLA, LII (1937), 390-397.

Durling, Dwight L. The Georgic Tradition in English Poetry. New York: Columbia University Press; London: Milford, 1935.

Empson, William. English Pastoral Poetry. New York: W.W. Norton, 1938.

Evans, B. Ifor. "The Eighteenth Century," Tradition and Romanticism. Studies in English Poetry from Chaucer to W.B. Yeats (London: Methuen, 1940), pp. 76-98.

Fairchild, Hoxie Neale. Religious Trends in English Poetry. Vol. II: 1740-1780, Religious Sentimentalism in the Age of Johnson. New York: Columbia University Press, 1942.

Fitzgerald, Margaret M. First Follow Nature. Primitivism in English Poetry, 1725-1750. New York: Kings Crown Press, 1947.

Friedman, Albert B. The Ballad Revival: Studies in the Influence of Popular on Sophisticated Poetry. Chicago: University of Chicago Press, 1961.

Fussell, Paul, Jr. Poetic Meter and Poetic Form. (Studies in Language and Literature, 3). New York: Random House, 1965.

Fussell, Paul, Jr. Theory of Prosody in Eighteenth-Century England. Connecticut College Monograph No. 5. New London: Connecticut College, 1954.

Garrod, H.W. *The Profession of Poetry and Other Lectures.* Oxford: Clarendon Press; New York: Oxford University Press, 1929.

Greene, Donald J. "'Logical Structure' in Eighteenth Century Poetry," PQ, XXXI (1952), 315-336.

Grierson, H.J.C., and Smith, J.C. *A Critical History of English Poetry.* London: Chatto and Windus, 1944.

Groom, Bernard. *The Diction of Poetry from Spenser to Bridges.* Toronto: University of Toronto Press, 1956.

Haas, C.E. de. *Nature and the Country in English Poetry of the First Half of the Eighteenth Century.* Amsterdam: J.J. Paris, 1928.

Hägin, Peter. *The Epic Hero and Decline of Epic Poetry.* (The Cooper Monographs, 8) Bern: Francke, 1964.

Halewood, William H. "'The Reach of Art' in Augustan Poetic Theory," *Studies in Criticism and Aesthetics, 1660-1800: Essays in Honor of Samuel Holt Monk*, ed. Howard Anderson and John S. Shea (Minneapolis, 1967), pp. 193-212.

Havens, Raymond D. *The Influence of Milton on English Poetry.* Cambridge, Mass.: Harvard University Press, 1922.

Herrick, Marvin Theodore. *The Poetics of Aristotle in England.* New Haven: Yale University Press; London: Humphrey-Milford; Oxford University Press, 1930.

Herrick, Marvin T. "The Place of Rhetoric in Poetic Theory," *Quarterly Journal of Speech*, XXXIV (1948), 1-22.

Hunt, Clay. "The Elizabethan Background of Neo-Classical Polite Verse," ELH, VIII (1941), 273-304.

Jack, Ian. *Augustan Satire: Intention and Idiom in English Poetry, 1660-1750.* Oxford: Clarendon Press, 1952.

Jones, Richard Foster. "Eclogue Types in English Poetry of the Eighteenth Century," JEGP, XXIV (1925), 33-60.

Jones, William Powell. *The Rhetoric of Science: A Study of Scientific Ideas and Imagery in Eighteenth-Century English Poetry.* Berkeley and Los Angeles, 1966.

Kliger, Samuel. "The Neo-Classical View of Old English Poetry," JEGP, XLIX (1950), 516-522.

Korshin, Paul J. "The Evolution of Neoclassical Poetics: Cleveland, Denham, and Waller as Poetic Theorists," ECS, II (1968), 102-137.

Kovacevich, Ivanka. "The Mechanical Muse: The Impact of Technical Inventions in Eighteenth Century Neo-Classical Poetry," HLQ, XXVIII (1965), 263-281.

Leavis, F.R. "English Poetry in the Eighteenth Century," Scrutiny, V (1936), 13-31.

MacLean, Norman. "From Action to Image: Theories of the Lyric in the Eighteenth Century," Critics and Criticism, Ancient and Modern, ed. R.S. Crane (Chicago: University of Chicago Press, 1952), pp. 408-460.

MacLean, Norman. "Personification but Not Poetry," ELH, XXIII (1956), 163-170.

Mace, Dean Tolle. "The Doctrine of Sound and Sense in Augustan Poetic Theory," RES, n.s., II (1951), 129-139.

Maddison, Carol. Apollo and the Nine: A History of the Ode. Baltimore: Johns Hopkins Press; London: Routledge, 1960.

Marsh, Robert. Four Dialectical Theories of Poetry: An Aspect of English Neoclassical Criticism. Chicago: University of Chicago Press, 1965.

Marsh, Robert. "Neoclassical Poetics," Encyclopedia of Poetry and Poetics, ed. Alex Preminger, Frank J. Warnke, and O.B. Hardison, Jr. (Princeton: Princeton University Press, 1965), pp. 559-564.

Martin, Abbott C. "The Love of Solitude in Eighteenth Century Poetry," SAQ, XXIX (1930), 48-59.

Miles, Josephine. "Eras in English Poetry," PMLA, LXX (1955), 853-875.

Miles, Josephine. Eras and Modes in English Poetry. Berkeley and Los Angeles: University of California Press, 1957.

Miles, Josephine. The Primary Language of Poetry in the 1740's and 1840's. (University of California Publications in English, Vol. 19, No. 2.) Berkeley and Los Angeles: University of California Press, 1950.

Miles, Josephine. "The Romantic Mode in Poetry," ELH, XX (1953), 421-424.

Moore, C.A. "Whig Panegyric Verse, 1700-1760: A Phase of Sentimentalism," PMLA, XLI (1926), 362-401.

Murray, Gilbert. The Classical Tradition in Poetry. (The Charles Eliot Norton Lectures.) Cambridge, Mass.: Harvard University Press; London: Milford, 1927.

Myers, Robert Manson. "Neo-classical Criticism of the Ode for Music," PMLA, LXII (1947), 399-421.

Neff, Emery. A Revolution in European Poetry, 1660-1900. New York: Columbia University Press, 1940.

Nethercot, Arthur H. "The Reputation of the 'Metaphysical' Poets During the Age of Pope," PQ, IV (1925), 161-179.

Nethercot, Arthur H. "The Reputation of the 'Metaphysical' Poets During the Age of Johnson and the 'Romantic Revival,'" SP, XXII (1925), 81-132.

Nevo, Ruth. The Dial of Virtue: A Study of Poems on Affairs of State in the Seventeenth Century. Princeton: Princeton University Press, 1963.

Nicolson, Marjorie Hope. The Breaking of the Circle: Studies in the Effect of the "New Science" upon Seventeenth-Century Poetry. Evanston, Ill.: Northwestern University Press, 1950.

Nicolson, Marjorie Hope. Newton Demands the Muse. Newton's 'Opticks' and the Eighteenth-Century Poets. (History of Ideas Series, No.2.) Princeton: Princeton University Press, 1946.

Nitchie, Elizabeth. "Longinus and the Theory of Poetic Imitation in Seventeenth and Eighteenth Century England," SP, XXXII (1935), 580-597.

Osgood, Charles Grosvenor. Poetry as a Means of Grace: Dante, Spenser, Milton and Johnson. Princeton: Princeton University Press, 1941.

Peltz, Catherine Walsh. "The Neo-Classic Lyric, 1660-1725," ELH, XI (1944), 92-116.

Press, John. *The Fire and the Fountain: An Essay on Poetry*. London: Oxford University Press, 1955.

Randolph, Mary Claire. "The Medical Concept in English Renaissance Satiric Theory: Its Possible Relationships and Implications," SP, XXXVIII (1941), 125-157.

Randolph, Mary Claire. "The Structural Design of the Formal Verse Satire," PQ, XXI (1942), 368-384.

Reaver, J. Russell. "The Retirement Theme: A Study of the Ways of Romanticism in Eighteenth-Century English Poetry," *Florida State University Studies*, III (1951), 63-90.

Reed, Amy Louise. *The Background of Gray's Elegy: A Study in the Taste for Melancholy Poetry, 1700-1751*. New York: Columbia University Press, 1924.

Renwick, W.L. "Notes on Some Lesser Poets of the Eighteenth Century," *Essays on the Eighteenth Century Presented to David Nicol Smith in Honor of his Seventieth Birthday*. (Oxford: Clarendon Press, 1945), pp. 130-146.

Richards, Edward Ames. *Hudibras in the Burlesque Tradition*. (Columbia University Studies in English and Comparative Literature, No. 127.) New York: Columbia University Press; London: Milford, 1937.

Sharp, Robert Lathrop. *From Donne to Dryden: The Revolt Against Metaphysical Poetry*. Chapel Hill, N.C.: University of North Carolina Press, 1940.

Sharp, Robert Lathrop. "Some Light on Metaphysical Obscurity and Roughness," SP, XXXI (1934), 497-518.

Shuster, George N. *The English Ode from Milton to Keats*. (Columbia University Studies in English and Comparative Literature, No. 150.) New York: Columbia University Press, 1940.

Smith, David Nicol. *Some Observations on Eighteenth Century Poetry*. (Alexander Lectures in English at the University of Toronto, 1937.) London and New York: Oxford University Press, 1937.

Spacks, Patricia Meyer. *The Insistence of Horror: Aspects of the Supernatural in Eighteenth Century Poetry*. Cambridge, Mass.: Harvard University Press, 1962.

Stewart, Keith. "Ancient Poetry as History in the Eighteenth Century," JHI, XIX (1958), 335-347.

Stewart, Keith. "The Ballad and the Genres in the Eighteenth Century." ELH, XXIV (1957), 120-137.

Stewart, Stanley. The Enclosed Garden: Tradition and Image in Seventeenth Century Poetry. Madison: University of Wisconsin Press, 1966.

Stone, P.W.K. The Art of Poetry, 1750-1820: Theories of Poetic Composition and Style in the Late Neo-Classic and Early Romantic Periods. London, 1967.

Stuart, Dorothy Margaret. "Landscape in Augustan Verse," Essays and Studies by Members of the English Association. Vol. XXV, 1940, Collected by Arundell Esdaile (Oxford: Clarendon Press, 1941), pp. 73-87.

Sutherland, James. A Preface to Eighteenth Century Poetry. Oxford: Clarendon Press, 1948.

Swardson, Harold R. Poetry and the Fountain of Light: Observations on the Conflict between Christian and Classical Traditions in Seventeenth Century Poetry. Columbia, Mo., University of Missouri Press, 1962.

Tillotson, Geoffrey. Augustan Poetic Diction. London: Athlone Press, 1964.

Tillotson, Geoffrey. "Eighteenth Century Poetic Diction," Essays and Studies by Members of the English Association, Vol. XXV, 1939 (Oxford: Clarendon Press, 1940), pp. 59-80.

Trickett, Rachel. "The Augustan Pantheon: Mythology and Personification in Eighteenth-Century Poetry," E&S, n.s., VI (1953), 71-86.

Trickett, Rachel. The Honest Muse: A Study in Augustan Verse. Oxford: Clarendon Press, 1967.

Trickett, Rachel. "The Idiom of Augustan Poetry," Discussions of Poetry: Form and Structure, ed. Francis Murphy (Boston: D.C. Heath, 1964).

Wallerstein, Ruth C. "The Development of the Rhetoric and Metre of the Heroic Couplet, Especially in 1625-1645," PMLA, L (1935), 166-209.

Wallerstein, Ruth C. Studies in Seventeenth-Century Poetic. Madison: University of Wisconsin Press, 1950.

Wasserman, Earl R. "Elizabethan Poetry 'Improved'," MP, XXXVII (1940), 357-369.

Wasserman, Earl R. *Elizabethan Poetry in the Eighteenth Century*. (University of Illinois Studies in Language and Literature, Vol. XXXII, Nos. 2-3.) Urbana, Ill.: University of Illinois Press, 1947.

Wasserman, Earl R. "The Return of the Enjambed Couplet," ELH, VII (1940), 239-252.

Wasserman, Earl R. *The Subtler Language: Critical Readings of Neoclassic and Romantic Poems*. Baltimore: The Johns Hopkins Press, 1959.

Weinberg, Bernard. "Scaliger versus Aristotle on Poetics," MP, XXXIX (1942), 337-360.

Wells, Henry W. "The Seven Against London: A Study in the Satirical Tradition of Augustan Poetry," Sewanee Review, XLVII (1939), 514-523.

Whelan, Sister M.K. *Enthusiasm in English Poetry of the Eighteenth Century (1700-1774)*. (Catholic University of America Diss.) Washington, D.C.: Catholic University of America, 1935.

Wilkinson, Andrew M. "The Rise of English Verse Satire in the Eighteenth Century," English Studies, XX (1953), 39-76.

Williams, George G. "The Beginnings of Nature Poetry in the Eighteenth Century," SP, XXVII (1930), 583-608.

Williamson, George. *The Proper Wit of Poetry*. London: Faber & Faber; Chicago: University of Chicago Press, 1961.

Wimsatt, W.K., Jr. "The Augustan Mode in English Poetry," ELH, XX (1953), 1-14.

Wimsatt, W.K., Jr. *The Verbal Icon: Studies in the Meaning of Poetry. And Two Preliminary Essays Written in Collaboration with Monroe C. Beardsley*. Lexington, Ky.: University of Kentucky Press, 1954.

Wyld, Henry Cecil. *Some Aspects of the Diction of English Poetry*. Oxford: Blackwell, 1933.

Youngren, William H. "Generality, Science, and Poetic Language in the Restoration," ELH, XXV (1968), 158-187.

V. The Other Genres: Fiction, Drama, Satire, etc.

Bateson, F.W. "Contributions to a Dictionary of Critical Terms:
1. Comedy of Manners," Essays in Criticism, I (1951), 89-93.

Bateson, F.W. English Comic Drama, 1700-1750. Oxford: Clarendon
Press; London: Mitford, 1929.

Berkeley, David S. "Préciosité and the Restoration Comedy of Manners,"
HLQ, XVIII (1955), 109-128.

Birkhead, Edith. "Sentiment and Sensibility in the Eighteenth Century
Novel," Essays and Studies by Members of the English Association,
XI (Oxford, 1925), 92-116.

Black, F.G. "The Technique of Letter Fiction from 1740 to 1800,"
Harvard Studies and Notes in Philology and Literature, XV (1933),
291-312.

Boas, Frederick S. An Introduction to Eighteenth Century Drama, 1700-1780. Oxford: Clarendon Press; New York: Oxford University Press,
1953.

Boyce, Benjamin. "The Effect of the Restoration on Prose Fiction,"
Tennessee Studies in Literature, VI (1961), 77-83.

Brie, Friedrich. Englische Rokoko-Epik (1710-1730). Munich: Max
Hueber, 1927.

Carlson, C. Lennart. The First Magazine. A History of the Gentleman's
Magazine with an Account of Dr. Johnson's Editorial Activity and of
the Notice given America in the Magazine. (Brown University Studies,
Vol. IV.) Providence: Brown University Press, 1938.

Clark, William S. "The Sources of the Restoration Heroic Play," RES, IV
(1928), 49-63.

Clinton-Baddeley, V.C. The Burlesque Tradition in the English Theatre
After 1660. London: Methuen, 1952.

Deane, Cecil V. Dramatic Theory and the Rhymed Heroic Play. Oxford:
University Press; London: Humphrey Milford, 1931.

Demott, Benjamin, "Comenius and the Real Character in England," PMLA,
LXX (1955), 1068-1081.

Dobrée, Bonamy. *Restoration Comedy, 1660-1720*. Oxford: Clarendon Press, 1924.

Dobrée, Bonamy. *Restoration Tragedy, 1660-1720*. Oxford: Clarendon Press, 1929.

Elliott, Robert C. *The Power of Satire: Magic, Ritual, Art*. Princeton: Princeton University Press, 1960.

Feinberg, Leonard. *The Satirist*. Ames, Iowa: Iowa State University Press, 1963.

Fujimara, Thomas H. *The Restoration Comedy of Wit*. Princeton: Princeton University Press, 1952.

Gagen, Jean Elizabeth. *The New Woman: Her Emergence in English Drama, 1600-1730*. New York: Twayne Publishers, 1954.

Graham, Walter. *English Literary Periodicals*. New York: Thomas Nelson & Sons, 1930.

Gray, Charles Harold. *Theatrical Criticism in London to 1795*. New York: Columbia University Press, 1931.

Green, Clarence C. *Neo-Classic Theory of Tragedy in England During the Eighteenth Century*. (Harvard Studies in English, XI.) Cambridge, Mass.: Harvard University Press, 1934.

Hamilton, K.G. *The Two Harmonies: Poetry and Prose in the Seventeenth Century*. Oxford: Clarendon Press, 1963.

Hanzo, Thomas A. *Latitude and Restoration Criticism* (Anglistica, Vol. xii.) Copenhagen: Resenkilde and Bagger, 1961.

Harvey-Jellie, W. *Théâtre Classique en Angleterre, dans l'âge de John Dryden*. Montreal: Beauchemin Limitée, 1933.

Hathaway, Baxter. "The Lucretian 'Return Upon Ourselves' in Eighteenth-Century Theories of Tragedy," *PMLA*, LXII (1947), 672-689.

Herrick, Marvin T. *Tragicomedy: Its Origin and Development in Italy, France, and England*. (University of Illinois Studies in Language and Literature, Vol. 39.) Urbana: University of Illinois Press, 1955.

Highet, Gilbert. *The Anatomy of Satire*. Princeton: Princeton University Press, 1962.

Hoy, Cyrus. "The Effect of the Restoration on Drama," *Tennessee Studies in Literature*, VI (1961), 85-91.

Kernan, Alvin B. *The Plot of Satire*. New Haven: Yale University Press, 1965.

Kitchin, George. *A Survey of Burlesque and Parody in English*. Edinburgh and London: Oliver and Boyd, 1931.

Krutch, Joseph Wood. *Comedy and Conscience after the Restoration*. New York: Columbia University Press, 1924.

Loftis, John. *Comedy and Society from Congreve to Fielding*. Stanford: Stanford University Press, 1959.

Loftis, John. "The Eighteenth Century Beginnings of Modern Drama," *Emory University Quarterly*, VII (1951), 225-236.

Loftis, John. *The Politics of Drama in Augustan England*. Oxford: Clarendon Press, 1963.

Loftis, John. "Spanish Drama in Neoclassical England," *Comparative Literature*, XI (1959), 29-34.

Lynch, Kathleen. "Conventions of Platonic Drama in the Heroic Plays of Orrery and Dryden," *PMLA*, XLIV (1929), 456-471.

McDonald, Charles O. "Restoration Comedy as Drama of Satire: An Investigation into Seventeenth-Century Aesthetics," *SP*, LXI (1964), 522-544.

McMahon, A. Philip. "Seven Questions on Aristotelian Definition of Tragedy and Comedy," *Harvard Studies in Classical Philology*, XL (1929), 97-198.

MacMillan, Dougald. "The Rise of Social Comedy in the Eighteenth Century," *PQ*, XLI (1962), 330-338.

Miller, Henry Knight. "The Paradoxical Encomium with Special Reference to Its Vogue in England, 1600-1800," *MP*, LIII (1956), 145-178.

Moore, Robert Etheridge. *Henry Purcell and the Restoration Theatre*. Cambridge, Mass.: Harvard University Press, 1961.

Muller, Herbert J. *The Spirit of Tragedy*. New York, Knopf, 1956.

Mylae, Vivienne. "Changing Attitudes Towards Truth in Fiction," *Renaissance and Modern Studies*, VII (1963), 53-77.

Nevo, Ruth. "Toward A Theory of Comedy," *JAAC*, XXI (1963), 327-332.

Prior, Moody E. "Poetic Drama: An Analysis and a Suggestion," *English Institute Essays, 1949* (New York: Columbia University Press, 1950), pp. 3-32.

Proper, C.B.D. *Social Elements in English Prose Fiction between 1700 and 1832*. Amsterdam: H.J. Paris, 1929.

Raysor, Thomas M. "The Downfall of the Three Unities," *MLN*, XLII (1927), 1-9.

Singh, Sarup. "Shakespeare and the Neoclassical Theory of the Drama," *Indian Journal of English Studies*, V (1964), 99-121.

Singh, Sarup. *The Theory of Drama in the Restoration Period*. Calcutta: Orient Longmans, 1963.

Smith, Dane Farnsworth. *The Critics in the Audience of the London Theaters from Buckingham to Sheridan: A Study of Neoclassicism in the Playhouse, 1671-1779*. (University of New Mexico Publications in Language and Literature, No. 12.) Albuquerque: University of New Mexico Press, 1953.

Stauffer, Donald A. *The Art of Biography in Eighteenth Century England*. Princeton: Princeton University Press; London: Humphrey Milford, Oxford University Press, 1941.

Stedmond, J.M. "English Prose of the Seventeenth Century," *Dalhousie Review*, XXX (1950), 269-278.

Steeves, Harrison R. *Before Jane Austen: The Shaping of the English Novel in the Eighteenth Century*. New York: Holt, 1965.

Sutherland, James R. and Ian Watt. *Restoration and Augustan Prose*. (Papers delivered at the third Clark Library Seminar, 14 July 1956.) Los Angeles: Clark Mem. Lib., UCLA, 1957.

Sutherland, James. "Some Aspects of Eighteenth-Century Prose," *Essays on the Eighteenth Century Presented to David Nicol Smith in Honour of his Seventieth Birthday* (Oxford: Clarendon Press, 1945), pp. 94-110.

Sutherland, W.O.S., Jr. *The Art of the Satirist: Essays on the Satire of Augustan England.* Austin, Tex., 1965.

Thorndike, Ashley H. *English Comedy.* New York, Macmillan, 1929.

Turner, Margaret. "'Natural Philosophy' and Eighteenth-Century Satire," *N&Q*, CXCVIII (1953), 296-299.

Tyre, Richard H. "Versions of Poetic Justice in the Early Eighteenth Century," *SP*, LIV (1957), 29-44.

Vines, Sherard. *Georgian Satirists.* London: Wishart, 1934.

Walker, Hugh. *English Satire and Satirists.* London: J.M. Dent; New York: E.P. Dutton, 1925.

Watt, Ian. *The Ironic Tradition in English Prose from Swift to Johnson.* Los Angeles: William Andrews Clark Memorial Library, 1956.

Watt, Ian. *The Rise of the Novel: Studies in Defoe, Richardson, and Fielding.* London: Chatto & Windus; Berkeley and Los Angeles: University of California Press, 1957.

Williams, Edwin E. "Dr. James Drake and the Restoration Theory of Comedy," *RES*, XV (1939), 180-191.

Wilson, F.P. *Seventeenth-Century Prose: Five Lectures.* Berkeley and Los Angeles: University of California Press, 1960.

Worcester, David. *The Art of Satire.* Cambridge, Mass.: Harvard University Press, 1940.

## VI. Literature and the Other Arts

Artz, Frederick B. *From the Renaissance to Romanticism: Trends in Style in Art, Literature, and Music, 1300-1830.* Chicago: University of Chicago Press, 1962.

Bronson, Bertrand H. "Some Aspects of Music and Literature in the Eighteenth Century," *Music and Literature in England in the Seventeenth and Eighteenth Century.* Papers delivered by James E. Phillips and Bertrand H. Bronson at the Second Clark Library Seminar, October 1953.) Los Angeles: Clark Library, 1954.

Davies, Cicely. "Ut pictura poesis," MLR, XXX (1935), 159-169.

Draper, John W. "Poetry and Music in Eighteenth Century Aesthetics," ES, LXVII (1932), 70-85.

Fehr, Bernhard. "The Antagonism of Forms in the Eighteenth Century." English Studies, XVIII (1936), 115-121, 193-205.

Fehr, Bernhard. "The Antagonism of Forms in the Eighteenth Century." English Studies, XIX (1937), 1-13, 49-57.

Folkierski. W. "Ut pictura poesis, ou l'étrange fortune du De arte graphica de Du Fresnoy en Angleterre," Revue de Litterature Comparee, XXVII (1953), 289-307.

Gilbert, Katharine. Aesthetic Studies: Architecture and Poetry. Durham: Duke University Press, 1952.

Gilbert, Katharine and Kuhn, Helmut. A History of Esthetics. New York: Macmillan, 1939.

Hagstrum, Jean H. The Sister Arts: The Tradition of Literary Pictorialism and English Poetry from Dryden to Gray. Chicago: University of Chicago Press, 1958.

Hollander, John. The Untuning of the Sky: Ideas of Music in English Poetry, 1500-1700. Princeton: Princeton University Press, 1961.

Hussey, Christopher. The Picturesque: Studies in Point of View. London and New York: G.P. Putnam's Sons, 1927.

Lee, Rensselaer W. "Ut pictura poesis: The Humanistic theory of Painting," Art Bulletin, XXII (1940), 197-269.

Malins, Edward. English Landscaping and Literature, 1660-1840. New York: Oxford University Press, 1966.

Music and Literature in England in the Seventeenth and Eighteenth Centuries. Papers delivered by James E. Phillips and Bertrand H. Bronson at the Second Clark Library Seminar, 24 October 1953. Los Angeles: William Andrews Clark Memorial Library, University of California (1954).

Rogerson, Brewster. "The Art of Painting the Passions," JHI, XIV (1953), 68-94.

Salerno, Luigi. "Seventeenth-Century English Literature on Painting," JWCI, XIV (1951), 234-258.

Schueller, Herbert M. "Correspondence Between Music and the Sister Arts, According to Eighteenth-Century Aesthetic Theory," JAAC, XI (1953), 334-359.

Schueller, Herbert M. "Literature and Music as Sister Arts: An Aspect of Aesthetic Theory in Eighteenth-Century Britain," PQ, XXVI (1947), 193-205.

Schueller, Herbert M. "The Use and Decorum of Music as Described in British Literature, 1700-1800," JHI, XIII (1952), 73-93.

Sypher, Wylie. Four Stages of Renaissance Style: Transformations in Art and Literature, 1400-1700. Garden City: Doubleday, 1955.

Tinker, Chauncey Brewster. Painter and Poet. Studies in the Literary Relations of English Painting. (The Charles Eliot Norton Lectures for 1937-1938.) Cambridge, Mass.: Harvard University Press, 1938.

Wellek, René. "The Parallelism Between Literature and the Arts," English Institute Annual, 1941 (New York: Columbia University Press, 1942), pp. 29-63.

Wittkower, Rudolf. "Pseudo-Palladian Elements in English Neo-Classical Architecture," JWCI, VI (1943), 154-164.

## VII. The Arts

Antal, Frederick. Classicism and Romanticism, With Other Studies in Art History. London: Routledge and Kegan Paul, 1966.

Antal, Frederick. "Reflections on Classicism and Romanticism, II," Burlington Magazine, March 1936, pp. 130-139.

Edwards, Ralph. English Conversation Pictures from the Middle Ages to about 1730: A Study in Origins. London: Country Life Press, 1954.

Evans, Joan. Pattern: A Study of Ornament in Western Europe from 1180-1900. 2 vols. Oxford: Clarendon Press, 1931.

Finney, Gretchen L. "Ecstasy and Music in Seventeenth-Century England," JHI, VIII (1947), 153-186.

Harman, Richard Alec and Anthony Milner. *Late Renaissance and Baroque Music (C. 1525-C. 1750).* (Man and his Music, 2) London: Barrie and Rockliff, 1959.

Hawley, Henry. *Neo-Classicism: Style and Motif.* Cleveland: Cleveland Museum of Art, 1964.

Hayward, John F. "Mimesis and Symbol in the Arts," *Chicago Review,* XV (1961), 93-106.

Honour, Hugh. "English Patrons and Italian Sculptors in the First Half of the Eighteenth Century," *Connoisseur,* CXLI (1958), 220-226.

Honour, Hugh. *Neoclassicism.* Harmondsworth: Penguin Books, Ltd., 1968.

Irwin, David. *English Neoclassical Art.* London: Faber, 1966.

Kaufman, Emil. *Architecture in the Age of Reason: Baroque and Post-Baroque in England, Italy and France.* Cambridge, Mass.: Harvard University Press, 1955.

Kristeller, Paul Oskar. "The Modern System of the Arts: A Study in the History of Aesthetics (II)," *JHI,* XIII (1952), 17-46.

Lang, Paul Henry. "The Enlightenment and Music," *Eighteenth-Century Studies,* I (1967), 93-108.

Leichtentritt, Hugo. *Music, History, and Ideas.* Cambridge, Mass.: Harvard University Press, 1938.

Mackerness, E.D. *A Social History of English Music.* London: Routledge and Kegan Paul, 1964.

Munro, Thomas. "The Psychology of Art: Past, Present, Future," *JAAC,* XXI (1963), 263-282.

Myers, Robert Manson. *Handel's Messiah: A Touchstone of Taste.* New York: Macmillan Co., 1948.

Newman, William S. *The Sonata in the Classic Era.* Chapel Hill: University of North Carolina Press, 1963.

Pach, Walter. "Art Must be Classical," *Virginia Quarterly Review,* XXVII (1951), 568-580.

Pevsner, Nikolaus. *Academies of Art Past and Present*. Cambridge: University Press, 1940.

Royal Academy of Arts. *British Tastes in the Eighteenth Century from Baroque to Neo-Classic: Winter Exhibition, 1955-6*. 2nd ed. London: Royal Academy of Arts, 1956.

Schueller, Herbert M. "The Pleasures of Music: Speculation in British Music Criticism, 1750-1800," *JAAC*, VIII (1950), 155-171.

Schueller, Herbert M. "The Quarrel of the Ancients and the Moderns," *Music and Letters*, XLI (1960), 313-330.

Siren, Osvald. *China and the Gardens of Europe in the Eighteenth Century*. New York: Ronald Press, 1950.

Southworth, James Granville. *Vauxhall Gardens: A Chapter in the Social History of England*. New York: Columbia University Press, 1941.

Spink, Ian. "English Seventeenth-Century Dialogues," *Music and Letters*, XXXVIII (1957), 155-163.

Summerson, John. *Georgian London*. New York: Scribner's, 1946.

Topazio, Virgil W. "Art Criticism in the Enlightenment," *Transactions of the First International Congress on the Enlightenment* (*Studies on Voltaire and the Eighteenth Century*, Vols. XXIV, XXV, XXVI, and XXVII), ed. Theodore Besterman (Geneva: Institut et Musée Voltaire, 1963), pp. 1639-1656.

Venturi, Lionello. *History of Art Criticism*. Translated from the Italian by Charles Marriott. New York: Dutton, 1936.

Waterhouse, Ellis K. "The British Contribution to the Neo-Classical Style in Painting," (Aspects of Art Lecture, read 3 March 1954), *Proceedings of the British Academy*, XL (1954), 54-74.

Whinney, Margaret, and Oliver Millar. *English Art, 1625-1714*. (Oxford History of English Art, ed. T.S.R. Boase, Vol.8.) Oxford: Clarendon Press, 1957.

## VIII. Texts and Anthologies

Adams, Henry Hitch, and Baxter Hathaway (eds.). *Dramatic Essays of the Neoclassical Age*, ed. Henry Hitch Adams and Baxter Hathaway. New York: Columbia University Press, 1950.

Bate, Walter Jackson (ed.). *Criticism: The Major Texts*, ed. Walter Jackson Bate. New York: Harcourt Brace and Company, 1952.

Berlin, Isaiah (ed.). *The Age of Enlightenment. The Eighteenth Century Philosophers*, selected with an introduction and interpretive commentary by Isaiah Berlin. New York: New American Library; Boston: Houghton Mifflin Co., 1956.

Boileau-Despreaux, Nicholas. *Selected Criticism*, translated, with an introduction by Ernest Dilworth. (Library of Liberal Arts.) Indianapolis: Bobbs-Merrill, 1965.

Boyce, Benjamin (ed.). *Prefaces to Fiction*. (Augustan Reprint Society, Pub. No. 32.) Los Angeles: Clark Memorial Library, University of California, 1952.

Bredvold, Louis I., Alan D. McKillop, and Lois Whitney (eds.). *Eighteenth Century Poetry and Prose*, ed. Louis I. Bredvold, Alan D. McKillop, and Lois Whitney. 2nd ed. New York: The Ronald Press, 1956.

Brinkley, Roberta Florence (ed.). *Coleridge on the Seventeenth Century*, with an Introduction by Louis I. Bredvold. Durham: Duke University Press, 1955.

Burrows, Leonard, and David Bradley (eds.). *Charitable Malice: A Choice of Augustan Satirical Poetry*. Nedlands: University of Western Australia Press, 1956.

Bysshe, Edward. *The Art of English Poetry (1708)*. With an introduction by A. Dwight Culler. (Augustan Reprint Society, Pub. No. 40.) Los Angeles: Clark Memorial Library, University of California, 1953.

Chapman, Gerald W. (ed.). *Literary Criticism in England, 1660-1800*. New York: Knopf, 1966.

Cobb, Samuel. "Discourse on Criticism" and "Of Poetry" from "Poems on Several Occasions" (1707). With an introduction by Louis I. Bredvold. (Ser. II: Essays on Poetry and Language, No. 1.) Los Angeles: Augustan Reprint Society, 1946.

Dacier, André. The Preface to Aristotle's Art of Poetry (1705), introd. by Samuel Holt Monk. (Augustan Reprint Society, Pub. No. 76.) Los Angeles: Clark Memorial Library, University of California, 1959.

Davie, Donald (ed.). The Late Augustans. London: Heinemann, 1958.

Elledge, Scott and Donald Schier (eds.). The Continental Model: Selected French Critical Essays of the Seventeenth Century, in English Translation. Minneapolis: Carleton College and the University of Minnesota Press, 1960.

Elledge, Scott (ed.). Eighteenth-Century Critical Essays. 2 vols. Ithaca, New York: Cornell University Press, 1961.

"Essay on wit" (1748); Richard Flecknoe's "Of one that zany's the good companion" and "Of a bold abusive wit" (second edition, 1665); Joseph Warton, "The adventurer," Nos. 127 and 133 (1754); "Of wit" ("Weekly register," 1732). With an introduction to the series on wit by Edward N. Hooker. (Ser. I: Essays on wit, No. 2.) Los Angeles: Augustan Reprint Society, 1946.

A full enquiry into the true nature of pastoral (1717). With an introduction by Earl Wasserman. (Ser. II: Essays on poetry, No. 4.) Los Angeles: Augustan Reprint Society, 1948.

Gilbert, Allan H. (ed.). Literary Criticism: Plato to Dryden, ed. Allan H. Gilbert. New York: American Book Co., 1940.

Hampshire, Stuart (ed.). The Age of Reason. The Seventeenth Century Philosophers, selected with an introduction and interpretive commentary by Stuart Hampshire. New York: New American Library; Boston: Houghton Mifflin Co., 1956.

Hearnshaw, F.J.C. (ed.). The Social and Political Ideas of Some English Thinkers of the Augustan Age. London: Harrap, 1928.

Hynes, Samuel (ed.). English Literary Criticism: Restoration and Eighteenth Century. New York: Appleton-Century-Crofts, 1963.

Jefferson, D.W. (ed.). Eighteenth-Century Prose, 1700-1800.
(The Pelican Book of English Prose, Vol. III.) Harmondsworth:
Penguin Books, 1956.

Morris, Corbyn. An Essay Towards Fixing the True Standards of
Wit, Humour, Raillery, Satire, and Ridicule (1744). With an
introduction by James L. Clifford. (Ser. I: Essays on wit,
No. 4.) Los Angeles: Augustan Reprint Society, 1947.

Needham, H.A. (ed.). Taste and Criticism in the Eighteenth Century:
A Selection of Texts Illustrating the Evolution of Taste and the
Development of Critical Theory. London: Harrap, 1952.

Poems on Affairs of State: Augustan Satirical Verse, 1660-1714.
New Haven: Yale University Press, v.d.
Vol. I, 1660-1678, ed. George de F. Lord, 1963.
Vol. II, 1678-1681, ed. Elias F. Mengel, Jr., 1965.
Vol. III, 1681-1685, ed. Howard H. Schless, 1968.
Vol. IV, 1685-1688, ed. Galbraith M. Crump, 1968.

Say, Samuel. An Essay on the Harmony, Variety and Power of Numbers
(1745), introd. by Paul Fussell, Jr. (Augustan Reprint Society,
Pub. No. 55.) Los Angeles: Clark Memorial Library, University
of California, 1956.

Sitwell, Edith (comp.). The Pleasures of Poetry: A Critical Anthology.
First Series: Milton and the Augustan Age. London: Duckworth,
1930.

Sutherland, James (ed.). Early Eighteenth Century Poetry. London:
Arnold, 1965.

White, Helen C., Ruth C. Wallerstein, and Ricardo Quintana (eds.).
Seventeenth Century Verse and Prose. Volume Two: 1660-1700.
New York, 1952.

Wood, Frederick T. (ed.) An Anthology of Augustan Poetry, comp.
and ed. Frederick T. Wood. London and New York: Macmillan,
1931.

## IX. Individual Authors

### Joseph Addison

Bloom, Lillian D. "Addison as Translator: A Problem in Neo-Classical Scholarship," SP, XLIV (1949), 31-53.

Elioseff, Lee Andrew. The Cultural Milieu of Addison's Literary Criticism. Austin, Tex.: University of Texas Press, 1963.

Friedman, Albert B. "Addison's Ballad Papers and the Reaction to Metaphysical Wit," Comparative Literature, XII (1960), 1-13.

Hamm, Victor M. "Addison and the Pleasures of the Imagination," MLN, LII (1937), 498-500.

Lewis, Clive Staples. "Addison," Essays on the Eighteenth Century Presented to David Nichol Smith in Honour of his Seventieth Birthday (Oxford: Clarendon Press, 1945), pp. 1-14.

Thorpe, Clarence D. "Addison and Hutcheson on the Imagination," ELH, II (1935), 215-234.

Thorpe, Clarence D. "Addison and Some of his Predecessors on 'Novelty,'" PMLA, LII (1937), 1114-1129.

Thorpe, Clarence D. "Addison's Contribution to Criticism," The Seventeenth Century: Studies in the History of English Thought and Literature from Bacon to Pope (Stanford, 1951), pp. 316-329.

Thorpe, Clarence D. "Addison's Theory of the Imagination as 'Perceptive Response,'" Papers of the Michigan Academy of Science, Arts and Letters, XXI (1936), 509-530.

Wheatley, Katherine E. "Addison's Portrait of the Neo-Classical Critic," RES, n.s., I (1950), 245-247.

### Mark Akenside

Aldridge, Alfred Owen. "Akenside and Imagination," SP, XLII (1945), 769-792.

## Archibald Alison

Kallich, Martin. "The Meaning of Archibald Alison's 'Essay on Taste,'" PQ, XXVII (1948), 314-324.

## Sir Richard Blackmore

Boys, Richard C. Sir Richard Blackmore and the Wits: A Study of "Commendatory Verses on the Author of the two Arthurs and the Satyr against Wit" (1700). (University of Michigan contributions in modern philology, No. 13) Ann Arbor: University of Michigan Press, 1949.

## Hugh Blair

Cohen, Herman. "Hugh Blair's Theory of Taste," Quarterly Journal of Speech, XLIV (1958), 265-274.

## Henry St. John, Lord Bolingbroke

Hart, Jeffrey. Viscount Bolingbroke: Tory Humanist. London: Routledge and Kegan Paul; Toronto: University of Toronto Press, 1965.

## Edmund Burke

Burke, Edmund. A Philosophical Enquiry into the Origin of our Ideas of the Sublime and Beautiful, ed. J.T. Boulton. London: Routledge and Kegan Paul; New York: Columbia University Press, 1958.

Bryant, Donald Cross. Edmund Burke and his Literary Friends. (Washington University Studies, Language and Literature, No. 9.) St. Louis, 1939.

## Samuel Butler

Quintana, Ricardo. "Samuel Butler: A Restoration Figure in a Modern Light," ELH, XVIII (1951), 7-13.

## Charles Churchill

Weatherly, Edward H. "Charles Churchill: Neo-Classic Master," UKCR, XX (1954), 266-271.

## William Collins

Woodhouse, A.S.P. "Collins and the Creative Imagination: A Study in the Critical Background of his Odes (1746)," Studies in English by Members of University College, Toronto (Toronto: University of Toronto Press, 1931), pp. 59-130.

## Abraham Cowley

Elledge, Scott. "Cowley's Ode 'Of Wit" and Longinus on the Sublime: A Study of One Definition of the Word Wit," MLQ, IX (1948), 185-198.

Nethercot, Arthur H. "Abraham Cowley's Discourse Concerning Style," RES, II (1926), 385-404.

Nethercot, Arthur H. "Concerning Cowley's Prose Style," PMLA, XLVI (1931), 962-965.

Walton, Geoffrey. "Abraham Cowley and the Decline of Metaphysical Poetry," Scrutiny, VI (1937), 176-194.

## William Cowper

Davie, Donald A. "The Critical Principles of William Cowper," Cambridge Journal, VII (1953), 182-188.

## George Crabbe

Crutwell, Patrick. "The Last Augustan," Hudson Review, VII (1955), 533-554 (on Crabbe).

Gregor, Ian. "The Last Augustan: Some Observations on the Poetry of George Crabbe (1775-1832)," Dublin Review, CCXXIX (1955), 37-50.

## John Dennis

Dennis, John. *The Critical Works of John Dennis*, ed. Edward Niles Hooker. 2 vols. Baltimore: The Johns Hopkins Press, 1939-43.

## John Dryden

Aden, John M. "Dryden and Boileau: The Question of Critical Influence," *SP*, L (1953), 491-509.

Aden, John M. "Dryden and the Imagination: The First Phase," *PMLA*, LXXIV (1959), 28-40.

Bredvold, Louis I. *The Intellectual Milieu of John Dryden. Studies in Some Aspects of Seventeenth-Century Thought.* Ann Arbor: University of Michigan Press, 1934.

Diffenbaugh, Guy Linton. *The Rise and Development of the Mock Heroic Poem in England from 1660 to 1714: Dryden's "MacFlecknoe."* Urbana, Illinois, 1926.

Dryden, John. *An Essay of Dramatic Poesy, A Defence of an Essay of Dramatic Poesy, Preface to the Fables.* Edited, with an Introduction and Notes, by John L. Mahoney. (Library of Liberal Arts.) Indianapolis: Bobbs-Merrill, 1965.

Dryden, John. *Of Dramatic Poesy and Other Critical Essays.* Edited with an Introduction by George Watson. (Everyman's Library, Nos. 568, 569.) 2 vols. London: Dent; New York: Dutton, 1962.

Eliot, Thomas Stearns. *John Dryden: The Poet, The Dramatist, The Critic.* New York: Holliday Bookshop, 1932.

Feder, Lillian. "John Dryden's Use of Classical Rhetoric," *PMLA*, LXIX (1954), 1258-1278.

Frost, William. *Dryden and the Art of Translation.* (Yale Studies in English, Vol. 128.) New Haven: Yale University Press, 1955.

Gardner, William Bradford. *The Prologues and Epilogues of John Dryden: A Critical Edition.* New York: Published for the University of Texas by Columbia University Press, 1951.

Hathaway, Baxter. "John Dryden and the Function of Tragedy," *PMLA*, LVIII (1943), 665-673.

Hoffman, Arthur W. *John Dryden's Imagery*. Gainesville, Fla., University of Florida Press, 1962.

Huntley, Frank Livingstone. *On Dryden's "Essay of Dramatic Poesy."* (University of Michigan Contributions to Modern Philology, No. 16.) Ann Arbor: University of Michigan Press, 1951.

Jefferson, D.W. "Aspects of Dryden's Imagery," *Essays in Criticism*, IV (1954), 20-41.

Joost, Nicholas. "Dryden's *Medal* and the Baroque in Politics and the Arts," *Modern Age*, III (1959), 148-155.

Ribner, Irving. "Dryden's Shakespearian Criticism and the Neo-Classical Paradox," *South Atlantic Bulletin*, XXI (1946), 168-171.

Roper, Alan. *Dryden's Poetic Kingdoms*. London: Routledge & Kegan Paul, 1965.

Spector, Robert D. "Dryden's Translation of Chaucer: A Problem in Neo-Classical Diction," *N&Q*, CCI (1956), 23-26.

Strang, Barbara, M.H. "Dryden's Innovations in Critical Vocabulary," *Durham University Journal*, LI (1959), 114-123.

Tillyard, E.M.W. "A Note on Dryden's Criticism," *The Seventeenth Century: Studies in the History of English Thought and Literature from Bacon to Pope, by Richard Foster Jones and Others Writing in his Honor* (Stanford: Stanford University Press, 1951), pp. 330-338.

Trowbridge, Hoyt. "The Place of Rules in Dryden's Criticism," *MP*, XLIV (1946), 84-96.

Turnell, G.M. "Dryden and the Religious Elements in the Classical Tradition," *ES*, LXX (1935), 244-261.

Van Doren, Mark. *The Poetry of John Dryden*. New York: Harcourt, Brace, 1920. 3rd rev. ed., 1946.

## Sir George Etherege

Underwood, Dale. *Etherege and the Seventeenth-Century Comedy of Manners*. (Yale Studies in English, 135.) Yale University Press; London: Oxford University Press, 1957.

## Henry Fielding

Bissell, Frederick Olds, Jr. _Fielding's Theory of the Novel_.
   (Cornell Studies in English xxii.)  Ithaca, New York:
   Cornell University Press; London:  Milford, 1933.

Radtke, Bruno. _Henry Fielding als Kritiker_.  Leipzig, Mayer & Müller,
   1926.

## John Gay

Brown, Wallace Cable.  "Gays Mastery of the Heroic Couplet," _PMLA_,
   LXI (1946), 114-125.

Mack, Maynard.  "Gay Augustan," _Yale University Library Gazette_,
   XXI (1946), 6-10.

## Thomas Gray

Griffin, M.H.  "Thomas Gray, Classical Augustan," _Classical Journal_,
   XXXVI (1941), 473-482.

Mell, Donald C., Jr.  "Form as Meaning in Augustan Elegy: A Reading
   of Thomas Gray's 'Sonnet on the Death of Richard West'," _PLL_,
   IV (1968), 131-143.

Starr, Herbert. _Gray as a Literary Critic_.  Philadelphia:  University
   of Pennsylvania Press, 1941.

Steuert, Dom Hilary.  "Two Augustan Studies," _Dublin Review_, CCXVI
   (1945), 61-74.  (On Gray.)

## Thomas Hobbes

Thorpe, Clarence D. _The Aesthetic Theory of Thomas Hobbes, with
   Special Reference to his Contribution to the Psychological
   Approach in English Literary Criticism_.  (University of Michigan
   Publications, Language and Literature, Vol. XVIII.)  Ann Arbor:
   University of Michigan Press, 1940.

David Hume

Brunius, Teddy. *David Hume on Criticism*. (Figura: Studies Edited by the Institute of Art History, University of Uppsala, No. 2) Stockholm: Almqvist & Wiksell, 1952.


Richard Hurd

Smith, Audley, L. "Richard Hurd's *Letters on Chivalry and Romance*," *ELH*, VI (1939), 58-81.

Trowbridge, Hoyt. "Bishop Hurd: A Reinterpretation," *PMLA*, LVIII (1943), 450-465.


Samuel Johnson

Babbitt, Irving. "Dr. Johnson and Imagination," *Southwest Review*, XIII (1927), 25-35.

Bate, Walter Jackson. *The Achievement of Samuel Johnson*. New York: Oxford University Press, 1955.

Brown, Joseph Epes. *The Critical Opinions of Samuel Johnson. A Compilation and Interpretation of Dr. Johnson's Principles of Criticism (Part One), and his Opinions of Authors and Works (Part Two)*. Princeton: Princeton University Press; London: Milford, 1926.

Brown, Stuart Gerry. "Dr. Johnson, Poetry, and Imagination," *Neophilologus*, XXII (1938), 203-207.

Christiani, Sigyn. *Samuel Johnson als Kritiker im Lichte von Pseudo-Klassizismus und Romantik*. ("Beiträge zur Englischen Philologie," Heft xviii.) Leipzig, Bernhard Tauchnitz, 1931.

Hagstrum, Jean H. "Johnson's Conception of the Beautiful, the Pathetic, and the Sublime," *PMLA*, LXIV (1949), 134-157.

Hagstrum, Jean H. "The Nature of Dr. Johnson's Rationalism," *ELH*, XVII (1950), 191-205.

Hagstrum, Jean H. *Samuel Johnson's Literary Criticism*. Minneapolis: University of Minnesota Press; London: Cumberlege, 1952.

Havens, Raymond D. "Johnson's Distrust of the Imagination," *ELH*, X (1943), 243-255.

Houston, Percy Hazen. *Doctor Johnson: A Study in Eighteenth Century Humanism*. Cambridge, Mass.: Harvard University Press; London: Milford, 1923.

Kallich, Martin. "The Association of Ideas in Samuel Johnson's Criticism," *MLN*, LXIX (1954), 170-176.

Kallich, Martin. "Samuel Johnson's Principles of Criticism and Imlac's 'Dissertation upon Poetry,'" *JAAC*, XXV (1966), 71-82.

Keast, William R. "Johnson's Criticism of the Metaphysical Poets," *ELH*, XVII (1950), 59-70.

Keast, William R. "The Theoretical Foundations of Johnson's Criticism," *Critics and Criticism Ancient and Modern*, ed. R.S. Crane (Chicago: University of Chicago Press, 1952), pp. 389-407.

Leavis, F.R. "Johnson and Augustanism," *The Common Pursuit* (London: Chatto and Windus, 1952), pp. 116-120.

Leavis, F.R. "Johnson as Critic," *Scrutiny*, XII (1944), 187-204.

McNulty, John Bard. "The Critic who Knew what he Wanted," *College English*, IX (1948), 299-303. (On Dr. Johnson as literary critic.)

Martyn, Howe. "Samuel Johnson, Critic of Poetry." *Queens Quarterly*, XXIX (1932), 425-450.

Mays, Morley J. "Johnson and Blair on Addison's Prose Style," *SP*, XXXIX (1942), 638-649.

Moore, Wilbur E. "Samuel Johnson on Rhetoric," *Quarterly Journal of Speech*, XXX (1944), 165-168.

Perkins, David. "Johnson on Wit and Metaphysical Poetry," *ELH*, XX (1953), 200-217.

Pyles, Thomas. "The Romantic Side of Dr. Johnson," *ELH*, XI (1944), 192-212.

Reynolds, W.V. "Johnson's Opinions on Prose Style," *RES*, IX (1933), 433-446.

Sachs, Arieh. "Generality and Particularity in Johnson's Thought," *SEL*, V (1965), 491-511.

Sato, Kiyoshi. "Principles of Criticism of Samuel Johnson," <u>Studies in English Literature, by the English Literary Society of Japan</u>, XXI (1941), 11-27.

Shackleton, Robert. "Johnson and the Enlightenment," <u>Johnson, Boswell, and Their Circle. Essays Presented to L.F. Powell</u> (Oxford, 1965), pp. 76-92.

Tate, Allen. "Johnson on the Metaphysicals," <u>Kenyon Review</u>, XI (1949), 379-394.

Watkins, W.B.C. "Dr. Johnson on the Imagination: A Note," <u>RES</u>, XXII (1946), 131-133.

Wimsatt, W.K., Jr. <u>The Prose Style of Samuel Johnson</u>. (Yale Studies in English, Vol. XCIV.) New Haven: Yale University Press; London: Humphrey Milford, Oxford University Press, 1941.

<u>John Locke</u>

MacLean, Kenneth. <u>John Locke and English Literature of the Eighteenth Century</u>. New Haven: Yale University Press, 1936.

Pahl, Gretchen Graf. "John Locke as Literary Critic and Biblical Interpreter," <u>Essays Critical and Historical Dedicated to Lily B. Campbell</u> (Berkeley and Los Angeles: University of California Press, 1950), pp. 137-157.

Smock, George E. "John Locke and the Augustan Age of Literature," <u>Philosophical Review</u>, LV (1946), 264-281.

Stolnitz, Jerome. "Locke and the Categories of Value in Eighteenth-Century British Aesthetic Theory," <u>Philosophy</u>, XXXVIII (1963), 40-51.

<u>George, Lord Lyttleton</u>

Rao, Amanda Vittal. <u>A Minor Augustan: Being the Life and Works of George, Lord Lyttleton, 1709-1773</u>. Calcutta: The Book Company, 1934.

## Andrew Marvell

Bradbrook, M.C. "Marvell and the Poetry of Rural Solitude," <u>RES</u>, XVII (1941), 37-46.

Brooks, Cleanth. "Criticism and Literary History: Marvell's Horatian Ode," <u>Sewanee Review</u>, LV (1947), 199-222.

Legouis, Pierre. <u>André Marvell, poète, puritain, patriote, 1621-1678</u>. Paris: Henri Didier; London: Oxford University Press, 1929.

Toliver, Harold E. <u>Marvell's Ironic Vision</u>. New Haven and London: Yale University Press, 1965.

## Alexander Pope

Adler, Jacob H. "Pope and the Rules of Prosody," <u>PMLA</u>, LXXVI (1961), 398-402.

Allen, Robert J. "Pope and the Sister Arts," <u>Pope and his Contemporaries: Essays Presented to George Sherburn</u>, ed. James L. Clifford and Louis A. Landa (Oxford: Clarendon Press, 1949), pp. 78-88.

Audra, E. <u>L'influence française dans l'oeuvre de Pope</u>. ("Bibliothèque de la <u>Revue de littérature comparée</u>," tome 72.) Paris: Champion, 1931.

Bickley, Francis. "Alexander Pope and the Lyrical Cry," <u>Sewanee Review</u>, XXXI (1923), 140-151.

Bishop, Carter, P. "General Themes in Pope's Satires," <u>West Virginia</u> University Bulletin: <u>Philological Papers</u>, VI (1949), 54-68.

Brower, Reuben Arthur. <u>Alexander Pope: The Poetry of Allusion</u>. Oxford: Clarendon Press, 1959.

Cameron, J.M. "Mr. Tillotson and Mr. Pope," <u>Dublin Review</u>, CCXXXII (1959), 153-170.

Goldstein, Malcolm. <u>Pope and the Augustan Stage</u>. (Stanford Studies in Language and Literature, 17.) Stanford: Stanford University Press, 1958.

Gress, Elsa. "The Culmination of Formalism in English Literature: Alexander Pope as Critic," Orbis Litterarum, II (1944-45), 293-301.

Hooker, Edward Niles. "Pope on Wit: The Essay on Criticism," The Seventeenth Century: Studies in the History of English Thought and Literature from Bacon to Pope, by Richard Foster Jones and Others Writing in his Honor (Stanford: Stanford University Press, 1951), pp. 225-246.

Jurgens, Heather. "'Windsor Forest' and Augustan Stability," Unisa English Studies, II (1967), 15-22.

Knight, Douglas. Pope and the Heroic Tradition: A Critical Study of his "Iliad." New Haven: Yale University Press; London: Cumberlege, 1951.

MacDonald, W.L. Pope and his Critics: A Study in Eighteenth Century Personalities. London: Dent; Seattle: University of Washington Press, 1951.

Mack, Maynard. "Secretum Iter: Some Uses of Retirement Literature in the Poetry of Pope," Aspects of the Eighteenth Century, ed. Earl R. Wasserman (Baltimore: The Johns Hopkins Press, 1965), pp. 207-243.

Mack, Maynard. "'Wit and Poetry and Pope': Some Observations on his Imagery." Pope and his Contemporaries: Essays Presented to George R. Sherburn, ed. James L. Clifford and Louis A. Landa (Oxford: Clarendon Press, 1949), pp. 20-40.

Morley, Edith J. "Joseph Warton's Criticism of Pope," MLN, XXXVI (1921), 276-281.

Moskovit, Leonard A. "Pope and the Tradition of Neoclassical Imitation," SEL, VIII (1968), 445-462.

"Alexander Pope. The Voice of Augustan England. Brilliance and Grandeur," TLS, 3 June 1944, p. 270.

Quennell, Peter. "Pope: An Augustan Portrait," Cornhill Magazine, CLIX (1939), 289-311.

Roberts, Michael. "Pope and English Classicism," Poetry Review, May-June 1930, pp. 161-170.

Stevenson, Samuel W. "'Romantic' tendencies in Pope," ELH, I (1934), 126-155.

Tillotson, Geoffrey. On the Poetry of Pope. Oxford: Clarendon Press, 1938.

Tobin, James E. "Alexander Pope and Classical Tradition," Bulletin of the Polish Academy of Arts and Sciences in America, III (1943), 343-354.

Toliver, Harold. "The Augustan Balance of Nature and Art in 'The Rape of the Lock', Concerning Poetry, I (1968), 58-69.

Tuveson, Ernest L. "An Essay on Man and 'The Way of Ideas'," ELH, XXVI (1959), 368-386.

Warren, Austin. "Alexander Pope," Rage for Order: Essays in Criticism (Chicago: University of Chicago Press, 1948), pp. 37-51.

Warren, Austin. Alexander Pope as Critic and Humanist. Princeton: Princeton University Press, 1929.

Wasserman, Earl R. "Pope's Ode for Musick," ELH, XXVIII (1961), 241-251.

Wimsatt, W.K., Jr. (ed.) Alexander Pope: Selected Poetry and Prose, ed. W.K. Wimsatt, Jr. (Rinehart Editions) New York: Rinehart, 1951.

Wimsatt, W.K., Jr. "Rhetoric and Poems: The Example of Pope," English Institute Essays, 1948, edited by D.A. Robertson (New York: Columbia University Press, 1949), pp. 179-207.

Matthew Prior

Spears, Monroe K. "Matthew Prior's Attitude Toward Natural Science," PMLA, LXIII (1948), 485-507.

Spears, Monroe K. "The Meaning of Matthew Prior's 'Alma'," ELH, XIII (1946), 266-290.

Spears, Monroe K. "Some Ethical Aspects of Matthew Prior's Poetry," SP, XLV (1948), 606-629.

Sir Joshua Reynolds

Macklem, Michael. "Reynolds and the Ambiguities of Neo-Classical Criticism," PQ, XXVI (1952), 383-398.

John Wilmot, Earl of Rochester

Erskine-Hill, Howard. "Rochester: Augustan or Explorer?" Renaissance and Modern Essays, XLVIII (1966), 51-64.

Thomas Rymer

Rymer, Thomas. The Critical Works of Thomas Rymer. Ed. Curt A. Zimansky. New Haven: Yale University Press, 1956.

Anthony Ashley Cooper, Third Earl of Shaftesbury

Alderman, William E. "Shaftesbury and the Doctrine of Benevolence in the Eighteenth Century." Transactions of the Wisconsin Academy of Sciences, Arts, and Letters, XXVI (1931), 137-159.

Alderman, William E. "Shaftesbury and the Doctrine of Moral Sense in the Eighteenth Century," PMLA, XLVI (1931), 1087-1094.

Aldridge, Alfred Owen. "Lord Shaftesbury's Literary Theories," PQ, XXIV (1945), 46-64.

Brett, R.L. "The Third Earl of Shaftesbury as a Literary Critic," MLR, XXXVII (1942), 131-146.

Brett, R.L. The Third Earl of Shaftesbury: A Study in Eighteenth-Century Literary Theory. London: Hutchinson, 1951.

Marsh, Robert. "Shaftesbury's Theory of Poetry: The Importance of the 'Inward Colloquy,'" ELH, XXVIII (1961), 54-69.

Stolnitz, Jerome. "On the Significance of Lord Shaftesbury in Modern Aesthetic Theory," Philosophical Quarterly, XI (1961), 97-113.

Tuveson, Ernest L. "The Importance of Shaftesbury," ELH, XX (1953), 267-299.

Tuveson, Ernest L. "Shaftesbury and the Age of Sensibility," _Studies in Criticism and Aesthetics, 1660-1800_, ed. Howard Anderson and John S. Shea (Minneapolis: Univ. of Minnesota Press, 1967), pp. 73-93.


Jonathan Swift

Beaumont, Charles Allen. _Swift's Classical Rhetoric_. Athens, Ga., University of Georgia Press, 1961.

Davis, Herbert. "Swift's View of Poetry," _Studies in English by Members of University College, Toronto_. (Toronto: University of Toronto Press, 1931) pp. 9-58.

Johnson, Maurice. _The Sin of Wit: Jonathan Swift as a Poet_. Syracuse, N.Y.: Syracuse University Press, 1950.


Sir William Temple

Marburg, Clara. _Sir William Temple: A Seventeenth Century "Libertin."_ New Haven: Yale University Press; London: Humphrey Milford, 1932.


James Thomson

Anwander, Erna. _Pseudoklassizistisches und Romantisches in Thomsons "Seasons."_ Leipzig: Bernhard Tauchnitz, 1930.

Cohen, Ralph. _The Art of Discrimination: Thomson's "The Seasons" and the Language of Criticism_. Berkeley and Los Angeles: University of California Press, 1964.

McKillop, Alan Dugald. _The Background of Thomson's Seasons_. Minneapolis: University of Minnesota Press, 1942.


Thomas Warton, The Younger

Havens, Raymond D. "Thomas Warton and the Eighteenth-Century Dilemma," _SP_, XXV (1928), 36-50.

## Edmund Waller

Allison, Alexander Ward. *Toward an Augustan Poetic: Edmund Waller's "Reform" of English Poetry.* Lexington, Ky.: University of Kentucky Press, 1962.

Chernaik, Warren L. *The Poetry of Limitation. A Study of Edmund Waller.* New Haven: Yale University Press, 1968.

## Horace Walpole

Chase, Isabel Wakelin Urban. *Horace Walpole, Gardenist: An Edition of Walpole's "The History of Modern Taste in Gardening" with an Estimate of Walpole's Contribution to Landscape Architecture.* Princeton, N.J.: Princeton University Press, for University of Cincinnati, 1943.

## Anne Finch, Countess of Winchilsea

Brower, Reuben A. "Lady Winchilsea and the Poetic Tradition of the Seventeenth Century," *SP*, XLII (1945), 61-80.

## William Wycherley

Zimbardo, Rose A. *Wycherley's Drama: A Link in the Development of English Satire.* (Yale Studies in English, No. 156.) New Haven and London: Yale University Press, 1965.

### X. Continental Background

Borgerhoff, E.B.O. *The Freedom of French Classicism.* Princeton: Princeton University Press, 1950.

Bray, René. "L'esthétique classique," *Revue des Cours et Conférences,* XXX (1929), 97-111, 211-226, 363-378, 434-449, 673-684.

Bray, René. *La Formation de la Doctrine Classique en France.* Paris, Hachette, 1927.

Clark, A.F.B. <u>Boileau and the French Classical Critics in England (1660-1830)</u>. ("Bibliothèque de la Revue de Littérature Comparée," No. 19.) Paris, Champion, 1925. Reprint, New York: Russell & Russell, 1965.

Folkierski, W. <u>Entre Le Classicisme et Le Romantisme: Étude sur l'Esthétique et les Esthéticiens du XVIII<sup>e</sup> Siècle</u>. Cracow: Académie polonaise des sciences et des lettres; Paris: Champion, 1925.

Hölzle, Erwin. <u>Die Idee einer altgermanischen Freiheit vor Montesquieu</u>. Munich and Berlin: Oldenbourg, 1925.

Hope, Quentin M. <u>Saint-Evremond: the Honnête Homme as Critic</u>. (Indiana University Humanistic Series, 51.) Indiana University Press, 1962.

Merian-Genst, Ernst. "Das Problem der Form in der französischen und Deutchen Klassik," <u>Germanisch-Romanische Monatsschrift</u>, XXVII (1939), 100-120.

Miller, John R. <u>Boileau en France au dix-huitième siècle</u>. (Johns Hopkins Studies in Romance Literatures and Languages, Extra Vol. XVIII.) Baltimore: Johns Hopkins Press: London: Humphrey Milford, Oxford University Press; Paris: Société d'édition Les Belles Lettres, 1942.

Moreau, Pierre. <u>Le Classicisme des Romantiques</u>. Paris: Plon, 1932.

Mornet, Daniel. <u>Histoire de la littérature française classique, 1660-1700: Ses Caractères Véritables, Ses Aspects Inconnus</u>. Paris: Armand Colin, 1940.

Peyre, Henri. <u>Le Classicisme français</u>, New York: Éditions de la Maison Française, 1942.

Peyre, Henri. <u>Qu'est-ce que le classicisme? (Essai de mise au point.)</u> Paris: E. Droz, 1933.

Tapie, Victor Lucien. <u>The Age of Grandeur: Baroque and Classicism in Europe</u>. Translated from the French by A. Ross Williamson. London: Weidenfeld & Nicolson; New York: Grove Press, 1960.

Tilley, Arthur. <u>The Decline of the Age of Louis XIV; or French Literature, 1687-1715</u>. Cambridge: Cambridge University Press, 1929.

Turnell, Martin. <u>The Classical Moment: Studies of Corneille, Moliere, and Racine</u>. Norfolk, Conn.: New Directions, 1948.

Van Tieghem, Paul. "Classique," <u>Revue de Synthèse</u>, I (1931), 238-242.

Van Tieghem, Paul. <u>Outline of the Literary History of Europe Since the Renaissance</u>. Translated from the French by Aimée Leffingwell McKenzie. With a preface by Ronald S. Crane. New York: Century Co., 1930.

Van Tieghem, Paul. <u>Precis d'histoire littéraire de l'Europe depuis la Renaissance</u>. Paris, Alcan, 1925.

Van Tieghem, Paul. <u>Le Préromantisme: Études d'Histoire Litteraire Européene</u>. (Second Series.) Paris: Alcan, 1930.

Wheatley, Katherine E. <u>Racine and English Classicism</u>. Austin: University of Texas Press, 1956.

Willoughby, L.A. "Classic and Romantic - A Reexamination," <u>German Life and Letters</u>, VI (1952), 1-11.

Wright, C.H.C. <u>French Classicism</u>. Cambridge, Mass.: Harvard University Press, 1920.

IOMS
10-12-71

## OHIO UNIVERSITY LIBRARY

Please return this book as soon as you have finished with it. In order to avoid a fine it must be returned by the latest date stamped below.

SEP 12 1973
DEC 17 1973
QUARTER LOAN
JUN 1 4 1992
APR 2 6 1992
JUN 1 3 2000

JUN 0 6 2000

CF